Marriage PLUS

THE BIBLE AND MARRIAGE

Ray Mossholder

Creation House
Lake Mary, Florida

Creation House
Strang Communications Company
600 Rinehart Road
Lake Mary, FL 32746
(407) 333-0600

First printing, October 1990
Second printing, December 1990
Third printing, December 1991
Fourth printing, September 1992

To my darlin' Arlyne.
This book has been written because of her faith in Jesus Christ
and in the author.

Acknowledgments

Years ago when one of the first televangelists, Bishop Fulton Sheen, received a television award for spontaneity, he spontaneously said, "I want to thank my four writers—Matthew, Mark, Luke and John!" Well, I want to thank them also, along with Paul, Peter, James and the writer of Hebrews. Oh, and all the Old Testament authors too. Without them this book could not have been written. Without God the Father, the Son and the Holy Spirit *no* book would have ever been written. Thanks!

As for others, the most important person in my life is my wife, Arlyne. We have a thrilling marriage, thanks to her. You'll find she's put some great thoughts in this book. With a super mom like her, it's small wonder our three grown-up kids, Tim, Bethany and David, turned out as they have. Wow, I'm a proud husband and dad!

Huge thanks to Oral Roberts University and Regent University (CBN) graduate Kirk Mitchell for the untiring work he did with me as I wrote this book. No one could be a more faithful friend. Kirk, my executive assistant, travels full-time with me. He patiently taught me how to use a computer. He did most of the statistical research for this book, spending hours holding a telephone in his hand. He would have stood on his head if I needed him to. Kirk wrote many of the vital questions at the end of each chapter, searching for the right scriptures. Our dialogue as we considered each question and verse prayerfully and his ability seemingly never to go to bed will not be forgotten.

Thanks to Mark and Debbi Linebarger, who one night during a seminar gave me my lap-top computer so that I could write this book. Without friends who financially give and pray as they do *Marriage Plus* wouldn't exist at all.

Very special thanks to Bill Gaultiere for many golden nuggets he's shared with me; I've inserted these throughout this book. Bill and his wife, Kristi, who also has her doctorate in psychology, are the authors of *Mistaken Identity: Clear Up Your Image of God and Enjoy Yourself,* published by Fleming H. Revell. If you haven't read it yet, do! It's powerful. Bill, a psychotherapist with the Minirth-Meier Clinic West in Orange, California, gave me a great deal of time and professional help with this book.

More words of praise for my "Your Money Matters" teaching friend, Malcolm MacGregor. His financial seminars save megabucks for all who attend. And for my longtime friends and accountants, Marshall and Bea Berman. Their Chatsworth, California, office has been a blessing to me ever since Marriage Plus began. Malcolm gave me great help in assembling a "Mom Bomb." All three helped me figure out what a "Mom Bomb" costs.

The vision and encouragement of the Marriage Plus ministry board have continually strengthened my hands. Thanks to president Wes Wilson, Jon Cook, John Zachman, Max Lile, the Rev. Jack Duitsman and Rob Buchheit—six great men who guide me faithfully.

My thanks to Gary Smith, Deanna Parris, Deborah Barber and Lane Arndt—my Marriage Plus office staff—for their prayers and great work that keep me wrinkle-free. Thanks also to our precious friend Dorothy Hedlund and to Dr. Tom Brussat, who helped Arlyne and me do the final editing of this book.

Thanks to the Rev. Don Sheley, who kept me from missing out on all that God has done. Thanks to Jack Hayford, my family's pastor for the last umpteen years, for telling me I "had to" write this book. Thanks also to David Gyertson at CBN, who even gave me a deadline.

Finally, a great big "God bless you" to Murray Fisher, Walter Walker, Rob McDonough and Debbie Cole of Creation House, who have patiently waited on the Lord and me. Writing a first book is like standing all alone on a stage and knowing everybody is watching you. Because of them and their encouragement and prayers, I have never felt alone.

All who have been in on my Marriage Plus or Singles Plus seminars know that I have been collecting thousands of jokes for the past twenty years. I can't be serious for too long or I fall over. One book stands out in this genre, and I quote from it often. Every pastor and speaker ought to own a copy of *14,000 Quips and Quotes for Writers and Speakers,* published by Baker Book House in Grand Rapids, Michigan. Thanks to them for so many ha-ha-has.

*"I will try to walk a blameless path,
but how I need your help, especially in my own
home, where I long to act as I should."*
Psalm 101:2, LB

"My people are destroyed for lack of knowledge."
Hosea 4:6, NASB

Contents

Dear Ray,

Now I know what the word despair means. I'm
in it! I am crying all day long and all night too. I
believe God hates divorce. He says that somewhere
in the Bible. But does God hate divorce as much as I
hate my marriage? I have to know, because I'm
dying inside. Your Marriage Plus seminars are
supposed to bring miracles into marriage. I've never
heard you speak or heard any of your teaching, but
I need a miracle. Got one up your sleeve for my
husband and me? I doubt it. But we sure need a
miracle, or I need a divorce.

Hopeless

*"Open my eyes
to see wonderful things
in your Word. I am but a pilgrim
here on earth: how I need a
map—and your commands are
my chart and guide."*

Psalm 119:18-19, LB

INTRODUCTION

If You Don't Have a Map, You're Lost

A THUMBPRINT ON THE BIBLE IS MORE IMPORTANT THAN A FOOTPRINT ON THE MOON!

"I don't care what you're going to say about marriage, Mossholder. I'm getting a divorce anyway!" The man spit the words in my face. If looks could kill, I would have been dead for sure. But by Friday night that man was holding his wife closely and repeating wedding vows he hadn't really meant on his wedding day.

Hundreds of divorces a year topple like Goliath during the Marriage Plus seminars I've taught around the world since 1979.

The Marriage Plus seminar, the only marriage seminar officially sponsored by Pat Robertson and the Christian Broadcasting Network, was born out of my absolute frustration. My wife's name, Arlyne, rhymes with darlin', but there was no "poetry" once we were wed. I hated my wife for the first twelve years of our marriage. Yet in 1971, while I was in Switzerland for a Christian conference, a miracle revived our marriage, though my wife wasn't even present. I discovered more than a thousand Bible verses on marriage that changed my life and hers.

Since then we've raised three children of our own and several teenagers from broken homes. They love Jesus Christ, and we all love each other too.

"Wait a minute," you may say. "Hold everything! I thought the 'happily ever after' and the 'white picket fence' were romantic fairy tales that ended after the honeymoon was over." Well, for far too many years that's what

I thought as well.

Don't Give Up Hope for Your Marriage

"Where there is no vision, the people are unrestrained" (Prov.
29:18)

Have you heard the story of the ant and the elephant? They were
childhood sweethearts. They loved each other so much that they wanted
to spend the rest of their lives together. (You've heard that love is blind,
haven't you?) On their wedding night they discovered that sex was
incredible. Neither the ant nor the elephant had ever felt so good. The
next morning the ant woke up and wanted to make love again. But, to
its horror, the ant discovered the elephant dead. Heartbroken, the ant looked
up to heaven and moaned, "Woe is me. Just one night of ecstasy, and
now I have to spend the rest of my life digging a grave."

There are countless married people like this poor ant: They married and
may have had some great moments together with their spouses. But now
they feel their marriages are dead.

So many Christians we encounter in our counseling and our speaking
ministry have given up hope that their marriages will ever be fulfilling.
What people say often reveals what is in their hearts:

"If only I hadn't married this person." (I picked a loser.)

"My spouse doesn't love me. No one has ever really loved me for who
I am." (I don't love myself.)

"If only she would get off my back and stop nagging me." (Maybe
it would be better if I were alone.)

"Maybe if I lost weight he'd desire me more." (It's my fault. I have
to change cosmetically, and then my spouse will love me.)

"There's no spark in our marriage, so I have to look for happiness
elsewhere." (I don't need this person anymore.)

"I do want a better marriage. But when my spouse doesn't seem to care,
what can I do?" (I've given up hope.)

"Why should I worry about having a happy marriage?" (I don't care anymore.)

Each of these sentiments is simply a variation on a theme: "I've given up hope for my marriage." (I don't believe God can bless my marriage.)

But I have great news for you: God isn't dead! God raised Jesus from the dead, so why not let Him raise your marriage out of the grave (where you've put it)? You may be able to see nothing but chaos in your marriage now, but God made this whole beautiful world out of chaos.

A billboard said simply, "Don't mope...Have hope!" What a great thought! If you don't have hope, you'll most likely mope. And no husband or wife wants to be around a Willie or Willimina Wimp. The Bible and psychologists agree that hope is the first step to receiving healing and moving forward in life. Jesus Christ is our hope (see 1 Tim. 1:1).

Our Lord told us,

> "Therefore everyone who hears these words of Mine, *and acts upon them,* may be compared to a wise man, who built his house upon the rock. And the rain descended, and the floods came, and the winds blew, and burst against that house; and yet it did not fall, for it had been founded upon the rock. And everyone who hears these words of Mine, and *does not act upon them,* will be like a foolish man, who built his house upon the sand. And the rain descended, and the floods came, and the winds blew, and burst against that house; and it fell, and great was its fall" (Matt. 7:24-27, italics mine).

Clearly, Jesus Christ says that there is *one way* to cause a shaky home to stand: to act upon the Word of God—the Bible. If we do as God says, our homes will be strengthened. God is looking for people who will obey Him (see 2 Chron. 16:9). His promises are beautiful, but they can be fulfilled only for those who will be "doers of the word, and not merely hearers [of it]" (James 1:22).

Today many good psychologically based books on marriage are available. Other fine books share wonderfully warm, personal experiences of marriages. These books offer some great tips on how couples overcame marital stress. But this book is different. Although two early chapters contain the story of my wife's and my first twelve stormy years of marriage and how God and His Word changed all that, the theme of this book is what God's

15

Word says about marriage. The devil is never afraid of a Bible with dust on it! With the very institution of marriage being threatened in America as never before, it is time for every person to blow the dust off the Bible and study the whole of God's teaching on marriage. While you're studying the written Word, you'll discover why the Creator of man, woman and marriage created them. You'll get to know the living Word (see John 1:14) much better too.

God's Word is clear: "Unless the Lord builds the house, they labor in vain who build it" (Ps. 127:1). If your hopes are to be real, they must be placed in God. To put your hope in God is to put your hope in the power of His Word to heal your marriage as you obey Him.

Our Lord told us, "Apart from Me you can do nothing" (John 15:5). Many churches have wonderful pastors and counselors available to give individual help to hurting people. And truly Christ-centered, Bible-focused psychologists should be applauded for the splendid help they offer. But people who go to counselors, psychologists or psychiatrists who don't guide by God's Word should have their heads examined.

God doesn't promise you a fairy-tale marriage. What He offers you is even better. Yet you can't expect to receive God's blessing in your marriage until you believe He *can* bless your marriage. And His blessings come by acting upon His Word.

Someone reading this may say, But I feel so much tension in my marriage I don't see how I can stay in it long enough to see a miracle. I say, Hold on. I say that because Jesus said, "If you abide in My word, then you are truly disciples of Mine; and you shall know the truth, and the truth shall make you *free*" (John 8:31-32, italics mine). Freedom doesn't come by getting a divorce but by acting upon His Word.

Every year since 1972 more than a million American couples have divorced. The facts are shocking:

- One in two American marriages is ending in divorce.
- Two in five first American marriages are ending in divorce.
- One in every three marriages is with someone who has already had at least one divorce.

It would be wonderful if the church could point to itself as the answer to marriage. But it can't. According to the National Opinion Research Center there is no appreciable difference between Protestant or Catholic divorce statistics and the statistics cited above. Almost every church in America is being rocked by divorce among its members. Even the clergy, with no permission from God, is doing it.

But it is one thing to be a hearer of the Word, another to be a preacher or teacher of the Word, and still another to be a doer of it!

The greatest tragedy is that nearly all these divorces are unnecessary. God has the answers. Christ is not the paralyzed Son at the right hand of His impotent Father. "Jesus Christ is the same yesterday and today, yes and forever" (Heb. 13:8); and He is at the right hand of His omnipotent (all-powerful) Father.

If you're looking for a glimmer of hope that your marriage can improve, here is good news: By discovering how to apply God's Word in your marriage, you can become like the wise and righteous pilgrim in Proverbs 4:18: "But the path of the righteous is like the light of dawn, that shines brighter and brighter until the full day." The glimmer of dawn is the sign of the full light the Son will shine on your marriage.

You say, "I don't see any hope." But God says, "Faith is...the evidence of things not seen" (Heb. 11:1, NKJV). And "if you have faith as a mustard seed [a very tiny seed]...nothing shall be impossible to you" (Matt. 17:20).

Arlyne and I are asking you to take our hands and let us guide you to your miracle. Your marriage may be in need of major repair, but so are a lot of houses that need the love and care of a handyman. What a waste to tear your marriage down when our Lord specializes in restoration.

> "Now may the God of hope fill you with all joy and peace in believing, that you may abound in hope by the power of the Holy Spirit" (Rom. 15:13).

A MARRIAGE LICENSE IS A HUNTING LICENSE FOR ONE DEAR ONLY!

Questions for Reflection and Discussion

1. List some of the times you know God answered your prayers in unexpected ways. Do you have the same hope and trust in God, believing He can answer your prayers concerning your marriage? Think about Abraham's

story as recorded in Romans 4:18-22. Meditate on Mark 10:27 and Ephesians 3:20-21.

2. Matthew 7:24-27 is one of the most important biblical passages on marriage. These verses clearly show the contrast between those who build a marriage that will stand and those who *choose* not to do so. What is the inevitable result of *not* building your marriage on the Word of God? Meditate on John 3:16-21; Romans 6:16; and Acts 3:22-23.

3. Look up the word *build* in the dictionary. Does building your house (marriage) upon the rock (Word of God) happen overnight, or is it a lifetime process? Meditate on Psalm 127:1 and Colossians 2:6-10.

4. Do you feel trapped in your marriage in the sense that you aren't free to be yourself? Meditate on 1 Corinthians 6:19-20; John 8:31-32; John 15:5; Psalm 119:32-35.

Dear Ray,

I'm crying as I write this short note to you. I thought marriage was going to be a fulfilling way to live. I'm thinking hard about divorce. My husband is a cantankerous, unkind, wretched louse. (And those are his good points!) He does things just to annoy me all the time. If I have a thought of my own, he puts me down and tells me he's got a lot better way of doing the same thing. I'm worried too that he may be having an affair. You say God doesn't allow divorce because a couple is incompatible. Well, we are—and I want out. Do you have anything to say that might keep me in?

Desperate

"Consider it all joy,
my brethren, when you encounter
various trials."

James 1:2

ONE

From Rock 'n' Roll to the Rock of Ages

**WHEN LIFE KNOCKS YOU ON YOUR KNEES,
YOU'RE IN A GREAT POSITION TO PRAY!**

At times an isolated verse of Scripture can seem absurd. Who but one with a twisted mind would rejoice in troubles? Yet God's Word is never foolish. God means what He says. He has, in James 1:2, written a clear instruction to each of His believers: Here's how to handle problems—rejoice!

Perhaps James 1:2 will make more sense to you if you answer this question: Would you like all of God's blessings on your marriage? Or, even more to the point, would you like miracles in your marriage? Well, there's a "catch" to receiving miracles: You have to have a problem to have a miracle. *The greater the problem, the greater the miracle!*

People can rejoice when they encounter trials for one reason: As they look to God with eyes of faith, they know they are headed for a miracle—no matter how bad things look where they are. Remember, "faith is the evidence of things *not* seen" (Heb. 11:1, italics mine).

In fact, like Paul and Silas, one can sing at midnight (see Acts 16:25) in spite of pain. One unchangeable law makes the present moment a time of rejoicing: "And we know that God causes all things to work together for good to those who love God, to those who are called according to His purpose" (Rom. 8:28). If you love God, you are called. No matter how bad the devil makes the picture look on your present canvas of life, you are headed for good if you keep following Jesus Christ and stay obedient to His directions.

James 1:2 is not actually a complete sentence. Let's look at it along with verse 3. "Consider it all joy, my brethren, when you encounter various trials, knowing that the testing of your faith produces endurance." When things go badly, and even following Christ doesn't seem to bring the immediate results you are believing for, you may cry out, "Why?"

Wouldn't it be great if every time we asked that question we heard a response like the one we hear over the radio: "This is a test. This is only a test. For the next sixty seconds...or two months...or twelve years...." But we never hear these words. Why not? Because we can read them. God *has* told us we will be tested for the faith we claim to have. As we saw in Matthew 7:24-27, there will be storms. You can count on it.

James said that testing "produces endurance." I can hear someone say, "I'd just as soon skip the endurance and not have the test, thank you." But endurance is absolutely necessary for you to see the fulfillment of God's promise to you. The devil, "the god of this world" (2 Cor. 4:4), will do everything in his power to make you believe you're going to lose. (It's a testing of your faith.) And the whole point is, every time you ultimately win against the devil, your faith grows. You are able to believe God for bigger and bigger miracles or blessings.

The thrilling news is you can count on Him for anything He promises in His Word. He'll give you what you're believing Him for or more— "beyond all that we ask or think" (Eph. 3:20). At your darkest moments it may not look as if He's going to come through. But don't mope; have hope. The best is yet to come!

James 1:4 identifies the "goal line" of the testing of your faith: "And let endurance have its perfect result, that you may be perfect and complete, lacking in nothing." Every time you believe God against unbeatable odds, you receive another miracle. Now will you believe for a miracle in your marriage? Will you endure all the way to the goal line?

From Marriage Minus to "Marriage Plus"

My girlfriend was dead, and I felt responsible. She and her brother had taken a shortcut to church on Sunday morning—because I wasn't with them. Anita had asked me to go to church with her, and I had said no. If I had been with them, they wouldn't have crossed those railroad tracks, and their car wouldn't have been hit. Anita was killed instantly.

I didn't know anyone could die at the age of sixteen. No one close to me had ever died. Grief and terrible guilt over not accepting her invitation to church prompted me to accept quickly her brother's invitation to First Baptist Church of San Jose that night.

The message by Clarence Sands seemed just for me. As he gave the altar call I went forward. I mumbled a prayer, asking Jesus Christ to come into my heart. After that prayer a lot of people slapped me on the back, telling me I was now "saved." With that many people saying it, I figured they couldn't all be wrong!

Since then I've carefully analyzed what happened that day. I was feeling great sorrow and guilt and I was shocked to realize that life on this planet does end. I had to do something to deal with the tremendous inner pain and emptiness. So I asked Jesus Christ to save me. The Lord knew my heart and the limitations I was placing on my relationship with Him. I wanted the "fire insurance" of salvation but not the decision-making lordship of Christ. The next several years would prove what a stupid mistake that really was.

After high school I entered Pepperdine College in Los Angeles. My major was speech and drama, but I actually majored in having fun. I was student-body vice president by my senior year. All notions of God were shoved to a back seat. By the time I graduated I had completely quit going to church.

At the age of twenty-two I had a high school teaching degree, and two things motivated my life. Lust—I wanted to go to bed with a woman. And loneliness—I was an extremely lonely guy.

Once I was home from college my mom insisted I start going to church again. I argued. Mom won. The first night back at First Baptist Church of San Jose, I met Arlyne Wegner. She was beautiful. (She still is!) She was also a deeply committed Christian who thought I was too. When Arlyne made it very clear that there would be no hanky-panky before marriage, I pressured her and unfairly rushed her to the altar. Six months after meeting her I married her. I wanted to get married so I could have sex with her, but two weeks later I realized I didn't really love her.

Opposites do attract. Arlyne's sex appeal had blinded me to how different the two of us really were. I was loud. She was quiet. I cluttered the house. She wanted everything organized and in its place. I wanted to slump. She wanted me to "sit up and get your hands out of your pockets." I wanted to spend money. She wanted to pay bills. I loved movies and television. She wouldn't have cared if either had never been invented. I cussed when I lost my temper. She was shocked by my words. On and on grew the list of complaints I had about my wife and she had about me. If I turned left, she turned right (and to me it seemed she thought she was always "right"). The more we disagreed, the more we argued; and the more we argued, the more I wanted a divorce.

For the next eight years I'd go to pastors and ask them, "How can I find love for my wife?"

They had one answer: "You've got to go back to what you felt at the beginning." I'd felt lust and loneliness at the beginning. I knew those feelings would not do me any good. They didn't!

We moved to Southern California. I took high school speech and drama teaching very seriously. I worked the kids hard, imagining I was on Broadway. I liked directing plays (being in charge with no arguments!). And I liked the kids (most of them seemed a lot friendlier than my wife). But most of all I liked the fact that my work kept me out of the house most of the time. Arlyne was teaching at an elementary school, and we were both so busy we had to schedule times to fight!

Once Arlyne married me, I felt little need to impress her with my "Christianity." The first year of marriage we slept in most Sunday mornings. But during the second year we met a Baptist pastor we liked who got us very involved in his church. We sang in the choir. Arlyne and I were in charge of the youth program, and I preached whenever the pastor was away. I knew hardly anything about the Bible, and my prayer life was shallow (often nonexistent); but I was a speech teacher, so I preached.

Plastic as my relationship with Christ was, I felt a tug at my heartstrings. I did feel a desire to know Christ. When, three years into our marriage, a seminary professor came to our church as interim pastor, I talked with him about my feelings. He helped me decide I should go to seminary—in the fall of 1962. What a disastrous year.

First, Arlyne continued working as a schoolteacher, while I worked at a J.C. Penney parking lot, making pennies! My manhood was severely challenged—she became my provider.

Second, and even worse, I was so confused by the philosophical arguments of liberal theologians that I nearly lost what very little belief in God I had. It never dawned on anyone to tell me, "The carnal mind doesn't understand spiritual things" (1 Cor. 2:14).

After that horrible year I quit seminary and went back to teaching school, hoping again to lose myself in my work. In spite of our unhappy marriage, Arlyne was pregnant. I told her I didn't want the child, as a baby would demand too much attention and take away our freedom. How wrong I was. One of the few wonderful memories I have of those years was our son Tim. I loved him from the first moment I held him in my arms. (I just didn't love his mother.) The instant bonding between Tim and me would be used by the Lord greatly to keep me in our marriage over the next rough years.

We moved back to the San Francisco Bay area the next year, and I continued teaching. But this school was full of undisciplined rich kids who wore me down. I enjoyed some of the students, but the routine rudeness made me lose my love for teaching.

On the home front uncivil war continued nightly. By the time Tim was four he was developing an ulcer because of the way Arlyne and I were fighting. The wounds we caused each other were verbal, not physical. But the pain of verbal abuse can seem as sharp as that caused by a fist or flying chair, and the effects of the abuse can be traumatic. Arlyne now tells women's groups that she was a nag. (I was a nag too, but what man wants to admit that?) Getting out of the house seemed the solution to our arguing. Divorce wasn't an option (pastors had told me that), so I hit upon the idea of moonlighting.

I didn't want a tough job. Speech and drama teaching were hard enough. I wanted a job that would be fun, and I found the perfect position at a rock 'n' roll radio station in Pittsburg, California. I was hired to be a commercial writer, but three days later the newsman got sick and the boss walked in: "Mossholder, get a newscast ready. You're going to be on the air in half an hour." My radio career was launched.

I loved doing the news. I did reports and interviews and worked my way into the midnight hours—completely avoiding my wife. The loose-as-a-goose life-style of a rock 'n' roll disc jockey appealed to me. So I was delighted a few months later when the boss told me he couldn't afford to pay me just to do the news; I was going to have to be a disc jockey too.

Now I played two parts: Ray Mossholder, the serious and level-headed newsman, and Barry Flynn, the wild, crazy disc jockey. In life I was playing two parts also: Religious Ray, the Sunday-morning churchgoer, and Ridiculous Ray, who drank, swore and partied with the rock-jocks.

Soon I quit going to church—when the boss assigned me the Sunday-morning shift.

Remember Hebrews 11:1: "Faith is...the evidence of things not seen"? Arlyne hung on in *faith*. She had every reason to quit; she was being abandoned. I usually came home late into the night. And I'd scoot out of the house as fast as I could in the morning. When I was home, all we did was fight.

My wife may have been a nag, but she also knew how to pray. She constantly prayed for me. I prayed for her, too, but my prayers were different from hers. She was asking the Lord to bring her prodigal husband back to Him. And I was praying for her to die! I actually did that many times! I rationalized that she would certainly want to get to heaven, and I wanted to get rid of her, so her death seemed the solution. I thank God now that He won't answer those kinds of requests.

Several months later I was amazed to get a phone call from the manager of a major radio network, who told me he'd been listening to my "news style." He thought I had real talent. He invited me to come interview with him. The interview went well, but the great job he had in mind for me wouldn't open up for a while. To break me in, he began using me as a freelance news reporter. At that point I quit my teaching position, keeping the job at the rock 'n' roll station.

In a few more months a Christian radio station contacted me. The boss there said, "Ray, we know you're a Christian." (I was a Baptist, so he reasoned I *must* be a Christian!) "We need a news director here at our station. Would you come?"

I didn't answer him immediately. Instead I phoned the network manager and said, "Look, I've just been offered a job as news director at a Christian radio station in San Francisco. But, of course, I could stay right here at this rock station. Which position would give me greater prestige with you when I join your network full-time?"

The manager answered, "By all means, go to the Christian station. San

Francisco is a major-market area. And you said news director? Both the city and the title will give you higher prestige with us."

With that high motivation, I took the job at the Christian station.

I want to stress that I didn't go there thinking I was a hypocrite. I thought I knew Jesus. Yet I knew Him much like the demon in Mark 1:24, which cried out, "I know who You are—the Holy One of God." I knew Jesus was the Holy One of God. "The demons also believe, and shudder" (James 2:19). But I wasn't even smart enough to shudder.

Someone has said, "Conceit is a strange disease. It makes everybody sick except the one who has it." But that statement is only partially true. Yes, everyone gets sick of a conceited person. But the conceited person is sick. I was sick—mentally and spiritually. A lesser physician would have called me a "terminal case." The Great Physician didn't!

Since I'd been a rock 'n' roll disc jockey, it was no great surprise that the manager of the Christian station wanted me to host a Christian teen show. "Spotlight on Teens" was designed to present Jesus Christ to teenagers and let them know that Jesus loved them. You may be surprised to know that a number of people came to Christ during the first thirteen months of that program—while I remained spiritually confused. But the Word of God does not return to Him void (see Is. 55:11). I was preaching the Word of God. (A jackass spoke the word of God in Numbers 22:28. I proved a jackass could speak the Word of God in our day too!)

Some theologians would say I was saved all during that time. Others would say I had fallen away. Some would say I'd never been saved. All I know is that I was interested in being a professional radio personality, not much interested in spiritual things and not at all interested in my marriage.

Thirteen months later the network manager phoned with an assignment. They had advance word of a protest in Port Chicago, California; two hundred university-aged kids would be lying down in front of napalm trucks and blocking them from the port. He asked me to do the exclusive radio coverage for them.

That day I interviewed everyone from a local police chief to the rioters. That night when I got back to the Christian station, the manager of the network called. "Ray, they're raving about you all over the network! Those Port Chicago stories were sensational. That job we've talked about is open now. Sixty thousand dollars to start. You'll do your own talk show. And we'll groom you for foreign correspondence. Welcome aboard, Ray!''

If you're looking for a miracle at this part of the story, it was that I was able to get my head in my car that night to drive home. I had a Volkswagen, and my head was so big!

I strode into our house and sneered at my wife, "We've made it! My name's going to be in lights. We're on easy street, baby. That big network has called. They're going to make me a world-famous newsman. Sixty thousand bananas to start!'' I went on and on and finally gloated, "Aren't you glad you're married to *me?*''

I was completely unprepared for her answer. She looked at me and said quietly, "Hello, Judas.'' I was stunned. "What do you mean, 'Hello, Judas'?''

"Well, for thirteen months you've been sitting on a Christian radio station saying, 'Come to Jesus. Come to Jesus.' And now that another station offers you a bag of silver, you're ready to sell out!''

No words I've ever heard have shocked me more. They were directly from the Holy Spirit through my wife. I was in deep pain for the next week. I had suddenly realized how hollow I was. I had been "selling" Jesus over the Christian station the same way I'd sold pizza and cars over the rock station. If I'd really believed all those things I was saying about Him, if I'd believed that telling others about Him was the most important thing a person could do, why was it so easy for me to quit now for "fame" and a "bag of silver"? I was as phony as I could be. And I suddenly hated it.

Something Happened

I love to hear the testimonies of people who have given their lives to Christ. The greatest testimonies are from those who were smart enough to choose Jesus Christ as Lord as far back as they can remember. But when, as in my case, a person doesn't really choose to follow Christ but tries to use Him as a rabbit's foot, the Lord often prepares a "pig pen" in which that prodigal son or daughter sees his or her wayward ways (Luke 15:11-24). One of the biggest mistakes often made by a person praying hard for his or her spouse to be saved is to tell God how the mate's salvation must occur. Arlyne never told God how. She simply stayed faithful to the Lord and me; she hung on to Him and would not let go. Hebrews 13:5b (Amplified) became her promise from God to give her security in the midst of our mess: "I will not in any way fail you nor give you up nor leave you without support. [I will] not, [I will] not, [I will] not in any degree leave you helpless, nor forsake nor let [you] down, [relax My hold on you]. Assuredly not!"

She claimed a second verse for both of us, Jeremiah 29:11 (LB): "For I know the plans that I have for you, says the Lord. They are plans for good and not for evil, to give you a future and a hope." If you are hurting right now, as you read Hebrews 13:5 and Jeremiah 29:11, accept them as God's promises to you too.

Actually, the "pig pen" God prepared for me was comfortable compared to many I've been told about. Three days after God spoke through Arlyne to me a research scientist from Stanford University phoned, inviting me to attend a gathering of "important Christian men" in the mountains of Santa Cruz. One of the men attending had helped invent the computer; another was the head of a large missionary organization; another, the pastor of a large church. I eagerly said yes I'd come—because I always liked being around big-named people. But when I hung up the phone I shouted at myself, "Dummy! Why did you say you'd go? You aren't going to have anything Christian to say to these men."

Fortunately, I didn't have to say anything. Those men did all the talking that Saturday. Man after man talked about what Jesus Christ was doing in his life—twenty-four hours of every day. I stayed silent. I figured there was no reason for me to speak up and show them how ignorant I was.

That night, as the men began to leave the gathering, I said to the man in charge, "Would you mind if I kept the key to this cabin? I'd like to stay here another day—and pray."

I'm sure that man was thinking, What a holy man this is! He wants to fast and pray. But as soon as those men were gone I knelt by the side of a bed and asked Jesus Christ to become Lord of my life. And God wrote the words I prayed indelibly on my heart so that I'd never forget them: "Lord, I don't even know if You exist." (I didn't, and I wasn't going to fake it anymore.) "But, if You *do* exist, I want to know You. The year 1968 is Your year, Lord. You can do anything in it You want to do. All I want to know, without a shadow of a doubt, is that You're *real.*" (I knew my performance was over. I could never continue being a phony or serve a phony god.)

At that moment Jesus Christ came into my life so that I knew it. I was alone in a cabin. No one slapped me on the back to tell me I was saved. My heart suddenly knew it, as sure as I know my own name. It didn't take a year to find out whether or not He was real. It took my declaring Him "Boss" of my life. (The word *Lord* means "Boss," and you can have only one God in your life—yourself or Him.)

When I walked into my house after Christ became real to me in that cabin, yet another miracle happened. For the first time in our marriage I cared about my wife. (I could say I "loved" her, but any comparison as to how I felt about her that night and how I feel about her now makes me use the word "cared.") I'd been wanting a divorce most days since we'd been married. I suddenly wanted our marriage to work. I wanted to be Arlyne's husband. *That was a miracle.* And Arlyne, whose prayer for me was suddenly being answered visibly, saw such a transformation in me that she made a deeper commitment to Christ in her life as well.

It was wonderful as we began our new life in Christ together. But the devil wasn't happy about it. That deceiver still had a big trick up his sleeve. Yet, though Satan planned evil against Arlyne and me, God meant it for good so that many people's souls and marriages could be saved. I'll tell you about it in the next chapter.

IT DOESN'T TAKE MUCH OF A PERSON TO BE A CHRISTIAN, BUT IT TAKES ALL THERE IS!

Questions for Reflection and Discussion

1. In light of James 1:2-4 think about some of the major trials you've faced. How did you handle those trials? List things you learned from these testings of your faith that have given you the ability to work through other problems. Are you rejoicing and praising God in the midst of any current trials? Read Acts 27-28 and note how Paul handled each test of his faith. Consider Paul's testimony in light of 1 Peter 1:6-9. Will you commit yourself to following Paul's example as a believer in Jesus Christ?

(See Phil. 3:17.)

2. When going through trials, we may not feel that God is with us. Did God promise that we would always "feel" His presence? What did He promise? Read Hebrews 10:35-36 in light of Hebrews 11:1. Memorize Hebrews 13:5 in the Amplified Bible: "He (God) Himself has said, I will not in any way fail you nor give you up nor leave you without support. [I will] not, [I will] not, [I will] not in any degree leave you helpless, nor forsake nor let [you] down, [relax My hold on you]. Assuredly not!"

3. Arlyne "endured." In James 1:4 what does the word *endurance* mean? Read Psalm 72:5 and Psalm 104:31 to get a clear picture of how long endurance can last. Read Mark 4:16-17 and 2 Timothy 4:3-4 to see why some people don't endure. Study Matthew 24:11-13; 2 Thessalonians 1:3-4; 2 Timothy 2:10; and James 5:10-11. For each passage, write down the blessings that come to those who endure.

4. Reread this chapter. Write down the mistakes I made and the mistakes Arlyne made. Married or single, what can you learn from our mistakes?

Dear Ray,

I'm in love. That probably sounds great to a guy who teaches marriage seminars. But I'm not in love with my husband. I'm in love with someone at my job. My husband doesn't know about it, but he'll probably find out soon. I want a divorce so I can marry the man I really love.

I married my husband for, well, convenience. I wanted to get away from my folks, and he seemed the best way to do it. I figured I'd grow to love him. Well, I haven't. He's no fun to be with, he's got a lot of habits I hate, and I don't think he loves me anyway. The only reason I haven't told him about the one I love is because we're Christians, and I don't know how he's going to react about getting a divorce. I think in his position at the church, and even in his career, he will feel he's exposed as a failure. I'm trying to be kind. But I'm in love, and the only way to marry the one I love is to divorce the one I don't. Makes sense, huh?

I know you gave up somebody you loved to stay with your wife. I'd like to know the details. What you did sounds crazy to me. Wasn't it crazy, Ray? I don't think what you say will make any difference. If you don't write me back I'll just go ahead with what I'm planning. But if you've got something to say that I'm not thinking about—say it. Thanks for even reading this letter.

In Love With Somebody Else

*"Again, the devil
took Him to a very high
mountain, and showed Him all
the kingdoms of the world, and
their glory; and he said to Him,
'All these things will I give
You, if You fall down
and worship me.' "*

Matthew 4:8-9

TWO

The Devil Offered Me the World

A 60-YEAR-OLD MAN HAS JUST MARRIED A 16-YEAR-OLD GIRL. NOW HE DOESN'T KNOW WHETHER TO TAKE HER ON A HONEYMOON OR SEND HER TO CAMP!

Empowered by the Holy Spirit, we began to find out how new and "abundant" life in Him can be. I just couldn't join the other network, as I wanted to tell everyone about Jesus Christ. But one evening as I sat doing the news on the Christian station, God further challenged my heart: "Ray, how do you know any of that news you read over the air is true?"

Embarrassed, I had to admit I couldn't know *any* of it was true. The news stories were written by people I didn't know, people who could have been honest or not.

Then God challenged me, "Why don't you share My 'good news'—which you *know* is true?"

And that's what I did. Resigning the news director's job, I kept the "Spotlight on Teens" program, by this time broadcast over five stations. Meanwhile, I became an associate pastor at a church, a Youth for Christ director, chaplain at a Salvation Army Booth home for unwed mothers and a youth pastor. God mightily blessed His call on my life. Within two years I was ministering to nearly a thousand teenagers each week in the San Francisco Bay area.

Our only daughter, Bethany, was born in June of 1968. There is something special in a dad's heart about having a daughter. She was a delight from the beginning.

When Bethany was ten months old we began to enlarge our family yet another way, taking most of Arlyne's time. We began taking teenagers into our home—girls whose own parents could not keep them.

With both of us "too busy," Arlyne and I began the loud, wretched arguments again, and this time I used "spiritual reasons" for abandoning her.

I was out of the house morning, noon and night for God. I spent so much time ministering, I had no time left to live what I lipped or walk what I talked. Although I had every good intention of becoming a great husband to my wife and a great father to my kids, I took no time to do it. Everything and everyone outside my home seemed more important to me than my family.

Acts 1:8 does *not* say, "You shall receive power when the Holy Spirit has come upon you; and you shall *do* My witnessing." No, Jesus Christ told His followers, "You shall receive power when the Holy Spirit has come upon you; and you shall *be* My witnesses." Somewhere in those busy two years I switched from being to simply doing. As I took my eyes off my Lord, the father of lies (see John 8:44) started talking to me clearly, and I began to listen.

While both young people and adults were coming to Christ every week through my ministry, I began to pay special attention to a lovely eighteen-year-old girl in our church youth group. It amazed me; she was so much more "spiritual" than my wife! She "understood me" so much more than Arlyne! I had bought Satan's lies hook, line and sinker.

On the surface it started out in a way that seemed innocent enough, but soon I began to violate every ethical code a Christian, let alone a Christian leader, must keep. I spent hour upon hour alone with her, talking with her on the phone, taking her places. I fell head over heels in love with her. She thought she was in love with me too. We wanted to marry. We had taken Satan's bait and were deceived.

Two years after the Lord had so powerfully transformed my life I walked into my house one day and said to my very pregnant wife, "I want a divorce." If I had kicked her, it wouldn't have come as more of a blow.

She cried hard. But then, that very day, she launched a "campaign in the Spirit" the likes of which I'd never seen. When I was out of the house she cried and prayed intensely for me. She stormed heaven. As soon as she knew I was on my way home she'd dry her eyes, put on fresh make-up and concentrate her love on me. Her nagging stopped. In spite of what I said or did, she loved me with God's unconditional love—emotionally and physically. That went on almost nonstop for thirty days. Every night I'd tell her this was the last night I'd be coming home. But every night there I was at home again.

This was a brand new wife, and I knew it. She had loved me throughout our marriage, but never like this. She completely caught my attention.

On the thirtieth day of my wife's diligent prayer, God moved powerfully: The senior pastor of the church where I served, Don Sheley of the Church of the Highlands in San Bruno (one of the wisest men I know), phoned me. "Ray, could I see you in the office tonight about eight? I've got some things I want to go over with you."

"Sure," I said. I knew I had nothing to worry about. I knew he didn't know anything about my girlfriend. I knew that until I walked into his office. There sat Arlyne. There sat my two best friends from the church. There sat all the church elders. There sat the pastor's father-in-law, who was also a pastor. Don said, "Sit down, Ray!" I sat down.

Something Pastor Sheley did next has powerfully opened one major part of our Marriage Plus ministry. He turned to all the elders in that room and said, "If any one of you breathes one word about this discussion, you'll be dismissed from eldership immediately!" That statement disarmed me totally. The pastor was giving me reason to trust these men. I knew that if I really repented, not only would Jesus Christ forgive me, so would they. Today I have the joy at times of going into situations much like my own that night and bringing healing to fallen pastors or their wives, just as healing was brought to my wife and me. Restoration, when it comes from Jesus Christ, doesn't take some certain amount of time that can be set by a human agenda. Restoration requires real repentance from the sinner, who will turn away forever from the sin, coupled with Christ's forgiveness and cleansing. In fact, the word *cleanse* means "total restoration"—as if a person had never sinned.

With that said, Don turned to me, and fire came from his Bible as he shouted, "You're *not* going to do this stupid thing you think you're going to do! You're *not* going to let your children go to hell because of the lust of their father! You're *not* going to let all those 'babes in Christ,' who believe in Jesus because of your ministry, spiritually shatter because you've suddenly become stupid! You're *not* going to do that!'' He opened his Bible and showed me verses like Matthew 7:21 and Hebrews 6:4-6.

"Ray," he continued, "what you're contemplating doesn't have so much to do with leaving Arlyne as it does with the walk you've established with Christ." That challenged me. Though I was deceived, I wanted to please Him. I knew what Pastor Sheley was saying was absolutely true.

Half an hour went by, and Don suddenly stopped and asked me, "Ray, do you know where the young woman you think you're in love with is? She's downstairs right now, repenting before the Lord."

I was furious, but there was nothing I could say or do.

Finally he said, "You're not going home tonight. Your wife has packed your bags. We're sending both of you to Springs of Living Water [at that time a Christian retreat center in northern California] so you can be away together. You won't have to worry about the cost; we're paying all of your bills here and at the retreat center. And don't worry about your children. We've made arrangements for them. You just get up there and get your act together."

He leaned even closer to me, looked straight into my eyes and said, "I don't care how long you stay up there...days...weeks...months...years! You two don't come back until you are both whole and your marriage is healed."

I was boiling mad. I stormed out the door, my wife following me, and I drove three-and-a-half hours to the Springs. Three-and-a-half hours of dead silence. I unloaded our luggage, banging it around, almost throwing it. I didn't want to be in that cabin, and without saying a word I let Arlyne know it. Every time she dared to talk, I froze her out. We went to bed in icy silence.

The next day I still wouldn't talk. Come evening, she went to bed early, and I stayed up. Trapped in my rage, I felt as if the cabin walls were smothering me. I was afraid—for myself, for the girl I'd left behind. If I didn't find something to occupy my mind, I was going to....

I reached into the suitcase and found a book Arlyne had planted there. I'd been reading it before my spiritual fall—Kenneth Wuest's commentary on 1 John. The Holy Spirit riveted my eyes on 1 John 1:9 (KJV): "If we confess our sins, he is faithful and just to forgive us our sins, and to cleanse us from all unrighteousness." I didn't want forgiveness, I wanted the girl! I slammed the book down, walked out the door and slammed it too.

Under a full moon I walked for at least half an hour. Pastor Sheley's words suddenly came back to me. "Ray, what you're contemplating doesn't have so much to do with leaving Arlyne as it does with leaving your walk with Christ." What would the "fallout" of my actions be?

That thought horrified me. Those last two years had been the best of my life, in spite of my marriage. I thought of teenagers I'd led to Christ, how they'd committed their lives to Him because I knew Him, and they knew I did. They'd spent hours with me, growing in Christ. I thought of four of them who joined me each week, ministering to the girls and young women at the home for unwed mothers. They were great kids. Some of them had come from sad backgrounds too. I'd become like a spiritual dad to them. Their lives were important for eternity, and I was suddenly concerned about what might happen to their walk with Christ if I walked out on my marriage. Why hadn't I thought about any of this before?

I thought about things I'd told those unwed mothers. Many of them hated men and were finding healing as they began to trust me. What would they think about my announcing what I was ready to do to my wife?

I thought of the teenage girls living in our home. They hadn't come from happy families; they looked to Arlyne and me as parental substitutes. They, too, were part of the youth group, which trusted me. I really did love them and care about what might happen to them if I walked out on my wife. What would it mean for their future? What would it mean for their walks with Christ?

I thought of the love Pastor Sheley had showed me and the trust he had in me. He had spent much time and money, not to mention prayer, to help me learn what ministry is. Even now, when it would have been so easy just to kick me out of the church and hold me up to public ridicule, he was spending still more money to help Arlyne and me. Could I really fail him now and make him a laughingstock?

And what about all my friends at the church? Was I willing to run the risk of giving some of them a reason to fall away?

And I thought of the girl I felt I loved. Could I give her up? I felt my marriage had been a hideous mistake from the beginning. I didn't love Arlyne. But this girl was everything I'd ever wanted. She and I had envisioned going right on with Jesus, laughing and loving, praying and ministering to the multitude. But would we? What would those who found out what we'd done really think? Ultimately, what would the Lord Jesus Christ say about my abandoning my wife and kids for her? I didn't know any scriptures about marriage. But I did know Matthew 7:21-23:

> "Not everyone who says to Me, 'Lord, Lord,' will enter the kingdom of heaven; but he who does the will of My Father who is in heaven. Many will say to Me on that day, 'Lord, Lord, did we not prophesy in Your name, and in Your name cast out demons, and in Your name perform many miracles?' And then I will declare to them, 'I never knew you; depart from Me, you who practice lawlessness.' "

So if I divorced my wife to marry this girl, what would I be doing to her and to me? I could rationalize and even twist Scripture to help me sear my conscience with a hot iron (see 1 Tim. 4:2). But what would I say to Jesus Christ on judgment day? Far worse, what would He say to us? I thought yet again of Pastor Sheley's words, "She's downstairs right now, repenting before the Lord." She was an honest Christian who loved the Lord. The truth hit: I had taken total advantage of her. Was I willing to keep on doing that? Maybe the Lord had gotten through to her with whoever counseled her, and she realized now how sinful I really was. Even if I did still love her, maybe she was smart enough not to love me anymore.

And I thought of my children. They were the hardest to think about. Again I remembered Pastor Sheley's words: "You're *not* going to let your own kids go to hell because of the lust of their father!" Would I do that? I thought about how hard it would be to ever convince them that Jesus Christ could meet their deepest needs if He hadn't met Mommy and Daddy's deepest needs and kept the family together. I pictured both Tim and Bethany. How deeply I loved them. Then I thought of the baby in Arlyne's womb. My child, whom I already loved. What influence was I having on it even now?

Suddenly I stopped. With tears in my eyes, I stared into the night sky and thought of what Jesus Christ had done on the cross for me. He'd suffered agony so that I could be freed from sin and its high cost. Was I willing to spit in His face and let all the people He had touched through me be jeopardized by hell itself? I knew the answer instantly. And I spoke to Him.

"Lord, I'm sorry. I've sinned against You. I've sinned against my wife. I've sinned against everyone who believes in You as a result of my witness. I have no more right to call You Lord. But I want to."

I paused. I thought hard for another moment. Was I willing to surrender? Was I willing to walk away from the forbidden love I'd found? If I told the Lord I'd stay in my marriage, could I keep the commitment? The Holy Spirit strengthened me and assured me that I could.

I continued to pray, "Lord, I surrender the girl. I promise I'll never see her again privately." (And I didn't. That was vital to my getting over her. Our relationship ended for me the moment I uttered those words. Fighting the feeling of "love" for her took two more years to burn out because the devil kept bringing surrendered feelings for her back into my mind.) "And I commit myself to my marriage—as long as the two of us shall live." (That was even harder to say because I knew I had to mean it, as well as everything else I'd said.)

There in the quiet God didn't speak, but I knew He'd heard me. He knew I meant every word I'd spoken. Then and there He forgave me. I thought of 1 John 1:9 once again. "If we confess our sins, He is faithful and just to forgive us our sins, and to cleanse us from all unrighteousness." In spite of all I'd done, I was clean.

I went back to the cabin and woke Arlyne. I said, "Honey, I'm sorry. I've been very stupid and very deceived. I've hurt the Lord, you and the kids. But I've just recommitted my life to Christ, and I've recommitted myself to our marriage. Can you find it in your heart to forgive me?"

She cried, and she forgave me.

We spent two more weeks at that cabin, trying to get our act together. Neither of us still knew much about marriage. We sure didn't know what to do to meet each other's needs. But we were determined to "tough it out."

When we went back to the church, no one had said a word about what I'd done; I was able to return to effective ministry with the total cleansing I'd received from the Lord. Immediately more teenagers and adults began coming to Christ. But for two years Arlyne and I still fought—and nagged. We clanged together like gongs! The Lord was allowing my commitment to Him to be tested to the limit.

You may be thinking, good grief, Ray, what does it take to get you straightened out? I've since learned that no matter how sincerely you repent or how committed you are to making your marriage work, you will still have problems—if you don't learn to live out God's plan for marriage.

A lot happened during those next two years. The high point was the birth of our last child, David. His sense of humor, even as a baby, kept needed laughter in our home.

The Lord moved us again to Southern California, where I took a job as a national representative for the worldwide missionary organization Youth With a Mission. In that capacity I traveled throughout the country. I stayed faithful to my wife. But we fought. Oh, we fought!

One day in 1970 Loren Cunningham, the founder and president of Youth With a Mission International, asked if I would participate in a minicongress on evangelism at the YWAM headquarters near Lausanne, Switzerland. I was delighted to accept his invitation.

The conference itself was wonderful. But for me the miracle occurred up in my room, "after hours" every night. There I began to search the Bible to find out what it said about marriage. For the past two years both Arlyne and I had been diligently praying for our marriage. I no longer prayed for my wife to die. Now I was praying for our marriage to live. Though our marriage was no longer terminal, it was sick, very sick. I needed answers. And now I burned the midnight oil to learn from God.

Marriage was God's idea in the first place. I reasoned that if God was the loving God I knew Him to be in every other way except my marriage, then marriage couldn't be a monstrous idea. Since He gave us the Bible to direct our paths (see Ps. 119:105), He must have put into His Word directions for marriage that would make the difference between happiness and misery. I wanted the "abundant life" Jesus Christ came to bring each of us (John 10:10). All we had was "abundant strife"!

The first passage of Scripture He showed me was Isaiah 55:6-10. The first two verses described what had happened to me two years before:

> Seek the Lord while He may be found;
> Call upon Him while He is near.
> Let the wicked forsake his way,
> And the unrighteous man his thoughts;
> And let him return to the Lord,
> And He will have compassion on him;

And to our God,
For He will abundantly pardon.

Then came the clearest description of why, in spite of salvation, the Holy Spirit, true repentance and prayer, my marriage wasn't working:

"For My thoughts are not your thoughts,
Neither are your ways My ways," declares the Lord.
"For as the heavens are higher than the earth,
So are My ways higher than your ways,
And My thoughts than your thoughts" (vv. 8-9).

Puny Ray had been trying to do things his way.

For two months I spent every spare minute in Switzerland studying everything God's Word says about husbands, *everything* it says about wives, *everything* it says about rearing children, *everything* it says about finances, sex, divorce. (I studied divorce especially hard because I was still looking for loopholes. I did find a very few, but none of them pertained to our marriage.)

Incompatibility is never biblical grounds for divorce.

I was amazed to discover that a spouse who loves Jesus Christ with all his or her heart, as did Arlyne and I, can be making as many mistakes as a sinner who ignores God—maybe even more. And it's happening because these people aren't *acting upon the whole Word of God* regarding *their* situations.

I would read about a husband, "A husband should...," and I'd think, I don't do that. And then I would read, "A husband shouldn't...," and I'd think, *That's* what I do!

As I continued to study, I found more than a thousand Scripture verses. And I began sending these home to Arlyne. I honestly wasn't "preaching at her," I just wanted her to share my discoveries. She got as excited as I was, and we both made new commitments to the Lord. She was in Southern California; I was in Lausanne, Switzerland, but each of us alone prayed a similar prayer: "Lord, forgive me. I thought I could have a great marriage without obeying Your Word. You know I didn't know Your Word about marriage. But now I see it. And, Lord, I promise, to the very best of my ability, to live Your directions for me. With Your power I can do it. Thank You for Your magnificent directions and thank You for forgiving me."

When I got home from Switzerland, I had a new wife. She had a new husband. We weren't suddenly perfect. It took a long time to practice all of God's directions. We're still practicing. But, oh, what an amazing difference God's directions made in our lives!

Someone may be raising this good question: Why, Ray, after you surrendered to the Lord and gave up the young woman, did you still have to suffer several more years of a painful marriage? I see three answers:

First, if the Lord had simply eliminated all pain the moment I surrendered, I would have never found the real answers. I would have simplistically thought confession was the whole answer. It isn't. *Acting upon God's Word* is the answer. And I still hadn't found God's directions for marriage.

Second, if the Lord had given me a perfect marriage the moment I surrendered, I might have fallen back into sin. Knowing me, I would have thought, Well, it's easy to get out of sin, so why not sin? I was sorely tempted. But once I'd burned my hand in the fire as an adult, I knew I'd be a fool to touch it again. As 2 Peter 2:22 bluntly puts it, " 'A dog returns to its own vomit,' and, 'A sow, after washing, returns to wallowing in the mire.' "

Third, in those two bad years so many incidents gave me greater understanding about marriage problems that I thank God for the problems themselves. The one major difference between me *before* the surrender and me *after* the surrender was that I really recognized the *why* behind many of our problems and worked like never before at solving them. I found a few could be solved by small changes of habits. But many, certainly many of the bigger problems (such as nagging), didn't go away, even with prayer. And they would have never gone away until Arlyne and I acted upon the Word.

Quite frankly, I am totally embarrassed about my past behavior. But I am so proud of my godly wife, who stayed faithful to me. And I am proud of my gracious Lord Jesus, who saved me and has taken my past failures and worked them out for good according to His promise in Romans 8:28.

I fully believe that the devil, as with our Lord (see Matt. 4:1-11) and with me, offers every Christian "the world" if he or she will just bow down to him. Perhaps the bigger the future opportunity, the bigger the prize he's willing to give. Had I accepted the world—or the eighteen-year-old, in my case—I would have lost the worldwide ministry the Lord has given me; thousands of families healed by His Word might easily be destroyed spiritually and emotionally today. What I'm sharing with you here is not just an interesting story but a warning: Whatever the devil offers in return for your worship, *don't bow down. You'll lose everything if you do.*

If you are hurting in your marriage even as you read this, please know that "God is our refuge and strength, a very present help in trouble" (Ps. 46:1). Arlyne and I urge you to pray the prayer we prayed so many years ago.

But, first, discover what I discovered in Switzerland. The rest of this book will outline much of what I found there. God wants to show you how to put His *plus* into your marriage.

WHEN YOU OBEY GOD'S WORD, NEVER BE AFRAID TO TRUST AN UNKNOWN FUTURE TO THE KNOWN GOD!

Questions for Reflection and Discussion

1. Has the devil ever offered you anything if you would disobey God's Word? What did he offer? Did you accept his offer or reject it? Study Romans 6:16-23. What is the reward of obedience to God? What is the cost of continued disobedience to God?

2. Satan is clearly identified as "the father of lies" in John 8:44. When speaking to women's groups, Arlyne often says, "The devil constantly disagrees with the Bible. If anyone else lied to you as the devil does, you wouldn't believe a word that person was saying. Well, why believe the devil's lies?" Arlyne's right. Jesus Christ came to give you "abundant life" (John 10:10), but Satan wants to steal, kill and destroy everything Jesus Christ came to do for you in your marriage and family. Are you going to let the devil do that to you? How can you stop him? The answer is in Ephesians 6:10-18. Make a list of "the whole armor of God" described in that passage. Do you constantly wear every piece of God's armor? If not, repent and tell the devil where to go!

3. I had fully committed my life to Jesus Christ as Lord in October 1967. Does it surprise you, as it did me, that I could subsequently fall away from His lordship? Compare Acts 1:8 with Matthew 7:21-23. What is the difference between "being Christ's witness" and "doing Christ's witnessing"? What could cause a committed Christian to switch from *being* to *doing?* Reread this chapter and write down the many mistakes I made that led to my deception.

4. Read Galations 6:1-2. The Greek word for *gentleness* is *praotes,* meaning "meekness." It is listed as one of the fruits of the Holy Spirit inside every Christian (see Gal. 5:23). *Meekness* means "great strength under God's control." Carefully reread the section about Pastor Sheley dealing with me and my sin. List the things that he did that showed how he fulfilled Galations 6:1-2. Arlyne and I are so thankful for what he did for us. How do you feel about his handling of our situation?

5. Arlyne loved me unconditionally for thirty days after she discovered I wanted a divorce. Read the first, fifth and seventh chapters of the book of Esther. By loving the way Esther did, Arlyne saved our marriage, and Esther saved the entire Jewish race. Write down the pros and cons of loving this way. Do you see any better alternatives for someone who really wants Christ to save his or her marriage? Should there be any "time limits" on such love?

Dear Ray,

I haven't told this to anyone at all. I am very confused, and someone heard your testimony and thought it might help me. Please send me your tape "God Can Heal Any Marriage." I just can't understand what's going on inside me. I'm sixty years old. I've gone to church since I was five years old. I have done just about everything—sung in the choir, taught Sunday school, passed out bulletins, been (and am) an elder....I've got a lot of my life tied up in church. But when I'm alone I get scared.

I'm not getting any younger. And here's the part I haven't told anybody: I don't know if God exists! Man, my pen shook when I wrote that. I'm scared because I don't want to think I've wasted my life and now am facing death with this uncertainty. That's why I want your tape of your testimony. I need to know what you did that changed your thinking. Please Federal Express that tape to me. I need to hear it fast. I'm tired of feeling empty inside while I tell everybody about Jesus. I'm tired of mumbling prayers that don't mean anything to me anymore.

A Churchgoer

"Not everyone who
says to Me, 'Lord, Lord,'
will enter the kingdom of heaven;
but he who does the will of
My Father who is
in heaven."

Matthew 7:21

THREE

Crown Him Lord of All

IT'S A TRAGEDY WHEN A "CHURCH" GIVES A "CHURCH VACCINATION" SO THE PEOPLE NEVER "CATCH" CHRISTIANITY!

On a Sunday morning an evangelist stressed his concern that so many in the church seemed to be sinning rather than winning: "There are two things paralyzing Christians and making them totally ineffective for changing the world's problems. The first is ignorance. The second is apathy." Staring at a man in the second row, he asked, "Isn't that right, sir?" The man answered quietly, "I don't know, and I don't care."

Ignorance (not knowing God's Word) and apathy (not caring what God says) *are* paralyzing vast sections of the church today. This is immediately recognizable among the marriages of churchgoers. Divorce is epidemic. Heartbreak is constant.

Divorce is even happening in record number among the clergy. Too often the ministry is no longer seen as a calling and profession of faith; it is simply a profession. The Bible is no longer *the* Book, but *a* book. The psalmist wrote, "Forever, O Lord, thy word is settled in heaven" (Ps. 119:89). But in too many minds it isn't "settled" down here on earth.

Colossians 2:8 clearly warns, "See to it that no one takes you captive through philosophy and empty deception, according to the tradition of men, according to the elementary principles of the world, rather than according to Christ." Though great Christ-centered Bible colleges and seminaries still exist, such schools must be carefully chosen, as students in many Bible

49

schools are finding their faith dying by degrees. The further they go in school, the more truth is being challenged by pseudo-intellectual professors who teach "philosophy and empty deception, according to the tradition of men." "Professing to be wise," these professors become "futile in their speculations, and their foolish heart [is] darkened" (see Rom. 1:18-22). Not honoring God, such schools are sending out so-called clergy who are as lost as the professors who taught them.

One churchgoer told me, "My pastor is a guy just like me. He tells dirty jokes, flirts with women and questions the Bible in almost every sermon. I don't know how his wife puts up with him...and he's all I know about the Christian life."

A double-minded clergyman who doubts the Bible (or refuses to obey it, as I did all the time I wanted the girl instead of my wife) is a terrible danger to himself and everyone who listens to him. Jesus Christ told the scribes and Pharisees, "Woe to you...hypocrites, because you travel about on sea and land to make one [convert]; and when he becomes one, you make him twice as much a son of hell as yourselves" (Matt. 23:15). It's a lot easier to argue the Bible than to obey the Bible. But the rewards of the two courses are altogether different.

Someone may ask, "But isn't there room in Christianity for honest doubt?" James answers,

> But if any of you lacks wisdom, let him ask of God, who gives to all men [and women] generously and without reproach, and it will be given to him. But let him ask in faith without any doubting, for the one who doubts is like the surf of the sea driven and tossed by the wind. For let not that man expect that he will receive anything from the Lord, being a double-minded man, unstable in all his ways (James 1:5-8).

Even those who do know God's Word will not follow it perfectly. Only Jesus Christ was perfect. The Christian who knows his or her imperfections and is working to correct them is as perfect as a person can get (see Heb. 5:13-14; Phil. 3:12-14).

But God won't accept "nobody's perfect" as a cop-out (see 1 John 2:3-4). On an airplane I sat next to a man who said, "I've quit going to church. So has my whole family. My pastor preached the Bible as if he were the apostle Paul himself. My wife, my kids and I loved him. We thought he was the closest thing to Jesus Christ on earth. Then one Sunday morning he gets up and preaches on 'all have sinned and come short of the glory of God.' Then he announces that he's resigning because he's had an affair with three women in the church. Can you believe it? Now he's out selling insurance, and we don't go to church anymore. How do you expect us to believe in Jesus Christ when a guy who supposedly knows Him so well does that?''

One of the tremendous joys I have in the Marriage Plus ministry is being called in to closed sessions with fallen pastors and their wives to bring healing to their homes and restoration to their churches. Repentance and restoration often come quickly, as they did with Arlyne and me. Other times a pastor refuses to repent. Second Corinthians 13:5 says to every falling pastor or believer, ''Test yourselves to see if you are in the faith; examine yourselves! Or do you not recognize this about yourselves, that Jesus Christ is in you—unless indeed you fail the test?''

With proper ministry to both the husband and the wife and proper safeguards by the elders, families of people like the man on the airplane don't have to become casualties in Christ. But unrepentance and a refusal to act upon the Word leave a spiritual battlefield strewn with casualties.

Where Do You Stand?

Mahatma Gandhi said, ''If Christians would live according to the teachings of Christ, all of India would be Christian today.'' Yet ''unbelieving believers'' are everywhere. The contradiction in terms would be laughable if it didn't carry such tragic consequences. People who hear the word of God but don't set their hearts on obeying it (see Matt. 7:26-27) drive people away from Christ. An agnostic challenged me recently, ''Ray, how can you seriously say that Jesus Christ is the answer to life? My folks dragged me to church as I was growing up, and they fought like cats and dogs. They didn't have any answers for life.''

A woman in honest confusion admitted, ''Ray, I came so close to asking Jesus Christ to save my soul. My boss at the office was making me excited about his 'relationship' with Jesus. He had me nearly convinced. Then one day while we were alone he grabbed me and tried to kiss me. Later he suggested we have dinner at a hotel. I turned him down. Yesterday he walked in and proudly announced he's getting a divorce. And I hear he's been sleeping with another girl in the office. How am I supposed to believe that Jesus is 'the way, the truth and the life'?''

Many churchgoers and even some pastors hear half a verse: Jesus Christ *is* "the way, and the truth, and the life" (John 14:6), but the sentence continues, "no one comes to the Father, but through Me." Jesus Christ is with His Father *now* (see Acts 2:31-33; 1 Pet. 3:18-22; Matt. 26:64). You can get to Father God only by following the One who is right beside Him. *Following Christ* is as essential as asking Him to save you—if you want to find the answers for your marriage, family and life (see John 8:31-32; 14:15; Acts 5:20; 1 Tim. 6:3-16; James 5:19-20). Failing to do that causes your Christian witness to sound stupid and be mocked by even your own spouse and children. You are the only "Bible" some of your friends will ever read. If you don't walk it as well as talk it, they will be confused about what it means to be a Christian.

Every person even considering becoming a Christian needs to understand that *no promise in the Word of God is automatically guaranteed. Every promise of God carries conditions that must be fulfilled if the Christian is to experience personally the fulfillment of the promise.* Even to become a Christian you must "confess with your mouth Jesus as Lord" (pray to receive the Lord) and "believe in your heart that God raised Him from the dead" (Rom. 10:9).

This does not mean that we are saved by works, "For by grace you have been saved through faith; and that not of yourselves, it is the gift of God; not as a result of works, that no one should boast" (Eph. 2:8-9). Bragging about being a great Christian because you are doing so much "for the Lord" doesn't impress anybody; it depresses both the Holy Spirit and those around you. Christ died for you. He purchased your salvation; you only have to receive what He's done for you (see Rom. 5:8-10). If someone invites you to an expensive restaurant and then pays the bill, you don't brag about how you treated him to dinner—unless you are a liar. Christ paid your bill in full when He went to the cross in your place; He purchased a banquet seat in heaven for you (see Rev. 19:9). Your bill is paid in full.

But any human can fail to understand what it means to believe his or her bill has been paid by Christ. Although we are not saved by our works, we will work if we really love Jesus Christ.

Lots of churchgoers don't like the book of James because it tends to louse up their "do-your-own-thing" philosophy. But in a day when every institution God founded—from the home to the church to the Christian faith itself—is being challenged by secular humanism, ignorance and apathy, we had better look closely at the whole story. James says:

> You believe that God is one. You do well; the demons also believe, and shudder. But are you willing to recognize, you foolish fellow, that *faith without works is useless?...You see that a man is justified by works, and not by faith alone....For just as the body without the spirit is dead, so also faith without works is dead* (James 2:19-20, 24, 26, italics mine).

Someone is bound to argue that the verses I've left out have to do with Old Testament illustrations. That's true. But James's point here centers on the New Testament illustration that in the Christian life faith and works always work together (see 2 Cor. 6:1). Far too many supposedly Christian husbands and wives are messing up the works!

So what happens to the faith that is a "gift of God"? Once again we face the danger of getting a piece of the truth but not peace from the truth— the whole truth. Following the beautiful and true promise that Christ paid the full price on Calvary for our sins (see Eph. 2:8-9) comes our call from the Lord: "For we are His workmanship, created in Christ Jesus for good works, which God prepared beforehand, that we should walk in them" (v. 10).

The Greek word translated as *workmanship* means "poem." You might say we were made to rhyme with God. When we are out of rhythm with Him, when we forget why we were made and lose the thrill of serving Him in all we do, we become the greatest losers in life. Everyone around us suffers.

We were made to serve God and also to do "good works." We don't do good simply to earn merit badges from God. Doing good is our very purpose in life, according to the One we'll meet face to face on judgment day, no matter where we're headed eternally (see 2 Cor. 5:10).

If you've been confused about what it means to be a Christian, it's time you re-examined God's Word and your life. It may mean the difference between life and death for you and for a lot of people you say you love (see 1 Tim. 1:18-19). Carefully read the promise of God for those who follow Him:

> If you abide [come and live in so that your outward actions reflect that you've been there] in My Word [the Bible], then you are truly disciples [believers] of Mine; and you shall know the truth, and [when you do it] the truth shall make you free (John 8:31b-32).

No one can become a Christian on his or her own terms. For the first eight years of my marriage, most of which were "churched," I repeatedly heard the words *Lord* and *lordship*. I nodded when I heard those words from the pulpit. (People usually nod when they're asleep.) I had no understanding of what the word *Lord* meant, nor did I care. As the saying goes, it was Greek to me.

When I finally asked Jesus to become my Lord, I still couldn't explain to anyone what *Lord* meant. But a few years later I went to Japan to do meetings. There it dawned on me. Their emperor had been called "Lord" for centuries. He was the one in charge, the head honcho, the unquestioned leader of Japan. Whatever he said went. When he told men to die for the glorious Land of the Rising Sun, they flew their planes into ships as kamikaze pilots and committed suicide. Small wonder they were such a military strength. But because their concept of *lord* wasn't biblical, the whole idea had been terribly distorted. Their lord had no Lord! A human being, not the Lord Jesus Christ, was calling the shots. No human, and no other god, can do that. Whenever anyone tries to replace the Lord of heaven with their own authority, there will be eventual, often immediate, disaster.

What is *lordship?* It is making Jesus Christ the One who is in charge, the unquestioned leader of your soul; doing this demands that you use the Word of God as the absolute guide for directing the steps of your life.

If God Seems Far Away, Guess Who Made the First Move?

Do you know that Jesus Christ is the Lord of your life? Do you want Him to be your Lord? If so, first recognize that no matter how successful your life seems to have been, your delay in asking Jesus Christ to be Lord of your life has caused a delay in the great things He has wanted to do in you and in your family. Your delay itself is sin. Until now you haven't known the purpose of your life. Now you will. You will be set free from the power of selfishness of sin and given the power to resist the devil and things that mar the joy of you and those around you (see 1 John 4:4). As you take this turn in your life, do three things:

1. *Speaking out loud, ask Jesus Christ to become Lord of your life.* Mean it. You might pray these very words:

> Dear Lord Jesus Christ, forgive me my sins. I want to know You. I want to follow You. Be my Savior and my Lord. I'll read Your Word. I'll believe Your Word. I'll do what Your Word says. Thank You for saving me and for giving me the power to follow You. You alone give eternal life. I'll follow You forever, Lord. Amen.

If you sincerely prayed this prayer, the Holy Spirit has come inside your spirit and turned you on.

Because Jesus Christ died on the cross in your place (see Rom. 5:8-11) to cancel your sins (see Is. 53:3-5; Col. 1:19-23), He is your Savior (see Titus 3:5-7) as well as your Lord (see Matt. 7:21).

Rejoice! All your previous sin is washed away in the blood of Christ, and He has given you the power to reject sin from now on (see 1 John 5:5-6). As far as your past—God can use anything to bring glory to Him (see Rom. 8:28).

Now tell another person that you've asked Jesus to be Lord of your life (see Rom. 10:9). I invite you to call my office and tell one of my staff. We will pray with you and answer your questions. Our office hours are 9 to 5 (Pacific Time), weekdays. Phone: 818-882-9424.

2. *Begin spending daily time in the Bible* (see 2 Tim. 2:15). Choose a version you can understand. Let God talk with you. Begin by studying one of the Gospels (Matthew, Mark, Luke and John). Ask the Lord which one you should read, and start with the one you feel drawn to. Throughout the coming year, read through the entire New Testament.

3. *If you are not already in a Christ-centered, Bible-believing church where the pastor knows Jesus Christ is alive and able to answer your needs as you follow Him, find one* (see Heb. 10:23-25). The pastor will be able to help you grow as a Christian, teaching you God's directions for the Christian life.

Christians are the light of the world, and God has just turned you on!

Questions for Reflection and Discussion

1. Colossians 2:6-8 tells all Christians to be firmly rooted, built up and established in Christ. It warns Christians to allow "no one" to take "you captive through philosophy and empty deception, according to the...elementary principles of the world." From Romans 1:18-22 and 2 John 5-11 determine how people get "captured" this way. How can you avoid this capture? Write down what you learn.

2. How perfect can a Christian become? Study Philippians 3:7-16 in light of Hebrews 5:12-14. What does *perfection* mean in the Christian life? After studying these passages, react to the statement (concluded from 2 Corinthians 5:10) that "doing good" is your purpose in life.

3. Read Mark 1:23-26 and James 2:19. Why does merely believing that Christ is "the Holy One of God" *not* make you a Christian? Read Romans 10:8-10. What does make you a Christian? Read Philippians 2:12-13. Is salvation a one-moment experience or a lifelong process?

4. Is it possible to be an "unbelieving believer"? Study Matthew 7:26-27 and James 1:19-25. If such a person exists, can he or she expect the blessings of God? (Read and act on 2 Corinthians 13:5.)

5. Study Philippians 3:8-10 and James 2:14-26. What is the difference between "grace" and "works"? Can you have one without the other? Find a complete concordance and note the number of times the words *Savior* and *Lord* are used in the New Testament. Can you have one without the other?

Dear Ray,

I am writing in total frustration. I heard your testimony, Ray. You say even for the two years after you surrendered your whole life and that girl you talk about to Christ, you and your wife "clanged together like gongs." Well, my wife and I have been doing that ever since we got married.

We love Jesus. But I can't take much more of this. We are exact opposites. If I'm thinking one way about something, you can jolly well bet she's going to be thinking the other way. Now she is crying a lot too. We didn't get in on your seminar. But would you please take mercy on me and give me any help you can in understanding why she's so opposite? Have I just married a loony-tunes or what?

Can't Figure Her Out

"...male and female
He created them."

Genesis 1:27

FOUR

Why Can't a Woman Be More Like a Man?

WOMEN'S FAULTS ARE MANY. MEN HAVE ONLY TWO: EVERYTHING THEY SAY, AND EVERYTHING THEY DO! —Anonymous

---

God created only two distinct sexes—and He did it on purpose. Like two pieces of a puzzle, they aren't the same, but they fit each other.

Despite attempts at "unisex," the differences between the sexes remain. The story is told of a man who gave a woman his seat on a bus; she fainted. When she revived, she thanked him; then he fainted.

When the differences between a man and woman are misunderstood and unappreciated, it spells marital disaster.

Many men can't imagine why God didn't bring a handball buddy or three poker-playing pals to Adam instead of a wife. At times nearly all men can identify with Professor Henry Higgins in *My Fair Lady*. In total frustration with the feminine ways of Eliza Doolittle, he sang, "Why can't a woman be more like a man?" A reprisal to that song could just as easily be sung by many a woman, "Why can't a man be more like a woman?"

A woman can talk with her mother on a telephone for twenty minutes. After she gets off the line, she's likely able to give her husband a "printout copy" of the conversation, nearly word for word. A man might talk with his mother for five minutes. When his wife asks what the mother said, he may simply answer, "She's fine." The different responses can cause misunderstandings. When you don't understand your spouse's actions, it's easy to blame the opposite sex for being so opposite.

It's easy, too, to blame God Himself for "messing up our lives." But blaming God is always wrong. His design is and always has been to bless the human race. Only when we fail to understand His purposes do we lose that blessing.

God makes it clear: We need both sexes (see 1 Cor. 11:12; Gen. 2:18; Rom. 1:24-27; 1 Cor. 6:9-11).

Before marriage, opposites attract. After marriage, a husband and wife begin to discover how very opposite they are. In those awful first twelve years of our marriage I often yelled at Arlyne about what had looked so great to me before we tied the knot. I had really liked how neat she kept everything. I'd go to her place for dinner and everything would be in place—exactly where it belonged. Her apartment could have passed the white-glove treatment. Not a speck of dust. And you should have seen the way she set the table. The shining plate, the knife, fork and spoon—right where they belonged. The napkin was folded just right—and the single rose.

How could I know that her attention to perfection would be offended at my keeping my clothes on the floor and everything I owned on top of my desk. Oh, did it offend her senses! But once at college, away from my mom, that's how I lived. My college dorm room was chaos corner. And my habits also brought a lot of chaos into my marriage too. But remember, before we married, I'd really admired how neat she was.

As for Arlyne? She'd seen me as a relaxed, fun-loving guy. She hadn't noticed that to me part of "relaxing" was never putting anything away. Opposites attract. After marriage, they attack!

Seeing Value in Your Differences

"And the man gave names to all the cattle, and to the birds of the sky, and to every beast of the field, but for Adam there was not found a helper suitable for him" (Gen. 2:20). Adam needed the human companionship of a wife. Hippos weren't enough. So God said, "It is not good for the man to be alone; I will make him a helper suitable for him" (Gen. 2:18).

Isn't it amazing? The only thing that wasn't "good" before the spiritual fall of Adam and Eve was Adam's aloneness, or loneliness, which is the real point of Genesis 2:18. All that God had created on earth—sun, moon, stars, sky, water, plants, trees, fish and animals—was "good" (see Gen. 1). But man without woman was not good.

And so God gave a divine anesthetic to Adam, took one of his ribs and gave him the girl of his dreams.

That man is incomplete without woman is literally true, as Eve was an "inside" job. Though lonely, Adam was complete until the day God took Eve out of him. Suddenly he was incomplete. Only when he saw her and she became his wife was Adam again complete. That's why he said, " 'This is now bone of my bones, and flesh of my flesh; she shall be called Woman, because she was taken out of Man' " (Gen. 2:23).

God has created us so that part of us is missing if we do not have a healthy relationship with the opposite sex.

If all this is true, you may be wondering if anyone can be "complete" without marriage. The answer is yes. In 1 Corinthians 7:7 the apostle refers to the gift of being single. But by the tragic amount of rampant sexual immorality evident in the single community, it is obvious that many have not understood or received this God-given gift. All Christian singles must "flee sexual sin" (see 1 Cor. 6:18-20). God totally condemns sex outside of marriage (see Heb. 13:4) and totally commends sex inside marriage (see 1 Cor. 7:2-5).

It is normal for a single adult to feel an ache inside for a marital relationship. However, too many people have discovered that the only thing worse than being single and lonely is being married and lonely.

God created men and women to be different from each other in many ways. And, as the French say, "Vive la difference!"

As you appreciate and learn from each other's differences, you are taking a big step in improving your marriage.

This chapter and the next discuss seven major differences between men and women. Warning: Don't get upset if your spouse doesn't—or you don't—fit all seven of these stereotypical differences, which are true about 80 percent of the time. In some cases you may categorize yourselves as being more like the opposite sex. But you'll probably find that the two of you do fit most of the stereotypical categories.

Seven Major Differences Between Most Men and Women	
Women	**Men**
1. Emotional (deeply caring)	1. Chauvinistic (cold logic)
2. Relationship-oriented	2. Work-oriented
3. Enjoy the process	3. Enjoy reaching the goal
4. Know by intuition	4. Know by analyzing
5. Physically weaker	5. Physically stronger
6. Often feel depressed	6. Often feel inadequate
7. Focused on the present and past simultaneously	7. Focused on the present or present and future

Difference 1:
Right-Brained Caring vs. Left-Brained Cold Logic

As I talk to couples I often hear, "He doesn't care about my feelings." Then the husband counters with, "All I hear from her is feelings. All I'm asking is that she be logical. She just won't listen to the facts." Why do they react so differently? Because the brains of males and females generally work differently. From cover to cover the Bible illustrates this fact in its coverage of men and women, husbands and wives.

In 1981 Dr. Roger Sperry won the Nobel Prize in medicine and physiology for his breakthrough study of differing brain functions in males and females. Although his study centered on epileptics, his information is insightful in keeping relationships friendly between any male and female. (For more help in understanding these differences read the books of Gary Smalley and Dr. Donald Joy.)

Dr. Sperry's work indicates that between the sixteenth and twenty-sixth week of gestation, boy babies have a chemical reaction that does not take place in girls. Literally, boy babies get a "chemical bath." Two chemicals are released that break down some of the fibers connecting the left side of the brain with the right side of the brain and slow down the development of the left side. (As Gary Smalley says in his seminars, "As all women already knew, all men are brain-damaged!")

What does this mean? Both sides of the brain still function. It is just harder for most males than females to use both sides of their brains at the same moment.

I'm happy to say that during the Marriage Plus seminars men often get more in touch with the right sides of their brains. But, even so, men and women still think differently.

So many marriage problems boil down to this one distinction: Women use both sides of their brains simultaneously, while men use one side or the other.

Let me stress: Men do get emotional, and women are often logical—sometimes far more logical than men. We've already agreed there are exceptions to these stereotypes. For example, 85 percent of male world-class musicians and artists are left-handed. And left-handed men are generally more "right-brained" than women.

On November 22, 1963, one of the most tragic events in American history occurred—the assassination of President John F. Kennedy. Anyone who was at least a teenager at the time can remember their own reaction to it.

The typical male reaction was: "President Kennedy is dead! Who's in charge of the country? What if Russia attacked right now?" With his left brain fully on alert, Lyndon Johnson was sworn in as the new president aboard Air Force One, even before he got to Washington, D.C.

But the typical female reaction was: "John Kennedy's dead! Oh, poor Jackie! Poor John-John and Caroline!" They wept for a widowed woman and her fatherless children.

Now neither the men nor the women were reacting foolishly. At such a time we need people concerned about both kinds of issues. One sex isn't bright and the other stupid. One sex isn't right and the other wrong. We need both kinds of thinking.

You might wisely ask if there are dangers to allowing either logic or emotions to determine our actions. The answer is yes. What many men call logic isn't logical at all. Consider Abraham sending his wife to a harem, thinking it, rather than trusting God, would save his skin (see Gen. 12:10-13, 20:9-13). The fact that God kept Sarah from sexual immorality shows His utter mercy.

On the other hand, the emotions can be misleading too. Feelings can lead to actions as ungodly as Abraham's pitiful logic. Michal—the daughter of King Saul and wife of King David—is a good biblical example.

In 2 Samuel 6:12-23 King David was thrilled to be bringing the ark of God home from the house of Obed-edom the Gittite, where "The Lord has blessed the house of Obed-edom and all that belongs to him, on account of the ark of God" (vs. 12). David's "logic" was hard at work: He knew he needed blessings on his own house, as his wife, Michal, was showing him no love at all, in spite of his need for her to stand with him.

Upon retrieving the ark, "King David [was] leaping and dancing before the Lord" (vs. 16). But Michal would have none of David's charismatic worship, feeling it was far too silly. She "looked out of the window and saw King David" worshipping God, and with every bit of bitterness she could muster, "she despised him in her heart" (v. 16). Michal was busy "judging" David (see Matt. 7:1-5).

David "returned to bless his household" (v. 20). But Michal, full of hate and led by her feelings, told her husband off and totally humiliated him (v. 20). Michal could have been one of the most loved women in history. Instead, she ended up totally rejected by David.

Some may argue that a clear study of Michal's bitterness shows good reasons why Michal was angry toward David (see 2 Sam. 3:12-18). But, in God's mind, forgiveness, not bitterness, is essential for any spouse who wants His blessings on the marriage (see 1 Cor. 13:4-5, Col. 3:19).

Pity Michal if you want to, but God had brought her to the palace. Once a person searches out God's Word on an issue and continues to act upon it (James 1:22-25), diligently prays (1 Thess. 5:17), resists the devil's temptations and refuses to sin (Eph. 6:11), keeps their faith fixed steadily on Christ in spite of what seems to be happening around them (2 Cor. 10:4-5), and walks in integrity before the Lord in full armor (Eph. 6:10-18), they need to accept the fact that God has put them where they are (Eph. 6:13). They need to expect God to change the outward circumstances in His perfect timing or deliver them from the circumstances. Michal had most likely waged no spiritual warfare. She just stayed mad. Her outrage at King David set up his spiritual fall. Since she obviously would never offer him her respect, he sinfully looked for respect in the arms of Bathsheba.

David had been remarkably insensitive. We can't whitewash this. And his "logical" command to bring Michal back to him after being separated for several years, years in which she had been wrongly given to another man while still married to David (see 1 Sam. 18:27), may have been more politically than romantically motivated. He thought restoring his marital claim on the daughter of the former king would strengthen his position for those who had loved Saul. Was David right in abandoning her for the rest of her life? No.

Neither ungodly emotional responses nor ungodly logical responses will lead to godly blessings. Here were two people responding with different sides of their brains, making terrible choices.

If neither logic nor emotion is a reliable motivator for right action, on what should we base our decisions and actions? There is only one correct answer: the Bible, or, more specifically, "acting upon" the Word of God (Matt. 7:24). Men aren't right. Women aren't right. But *God is always right.* The battle of the sexes (which has been with us ever since Adam and Eve) can only rightly end in acting upon the Word of God because God is always right.

"Therefore everyone who hears these words of Mine, and acts upon them, may be compared to a wise man, who built his house upon the rock" (Matt. 7:24).

Difference 2:
Relationships vs. Work

A pattern that appears often in the New Testament is obvious in this verse: "Nevertheless let each individual among you also love his own wife even as himself; and let the wife see to it that she respect her husband" (Eph. 5:33).

The apostle Paul could have lumped both husbands and wives together by simply telling them to love and respect each other. But he didn't. He has clearly separated them and the specific action each is to have toward his or her mate: Husband..."love" your wife. Wife..."respect" your husband.

Paul has addressed husbands and wives separately because men and women have different primary needs.

Women, with their bilateral thinking (the left side of the brain being heavily affected by the right side), are usually more relationship-oriented, as the desire for close relationships is found in the right side of the brain. Men, on the other hand, being more unilateral, are far more interested in winning and conquering.

In short, a wife needs to be loved (closely and meaningfully related to) by her husband. A husband needs to be respected by his wife (making him feel like a winner).

Most women, far more interested in relationships than most men, are like built-in sensors, their feelings tuned in to the status of any relationship. They sense how things are going between themselves and others. What makes women sad? Feeling lonely or unloved.

On the other hand, men need to have something to accomplish (and someone to notice they've accomplished it) if they are going to feel worthwhile and good about themselves. Take notice of his accomplishments and tell a man how well he's done, and you'll get somewhere with him. What upsets a man? Feeling insignificant or thinking himself a failure.

Husbands, what does your wife need to hear from you? "I love you. It's so good to be with you. You're so much fun. You're such a good mother and make our home so comfortable. You've been working so hard. You rest, and I'll wash the dishes." And wives, what does your husband want to hear? "Wow, you did a great job, honey! I'm so proud of you. You are so talented, thoughtful, hard-working, handsome, fun to be with...."

"Whoa," you may be saying. "But I don't feel any love for her. I've quit caring about her." Or, "Are you kidding? My husband sits around the house all day and doesn't have a talented bone in his body. A gorilla is more handsome than he is!" Then from both mouths comes the line that has probably killed more marriages than any other: "When he (or she) changes and works to meet my needs, *then* I'll work to meet his (or hers)."

Bill Gaultiere counseled a couple with supposedly irreconcilable differences (translation: "a deadlock of selfishness"). Jack and Kim were committed Christians on the verge of divorce. Seeing Bill was their last grasp for help. Except for his Christian faith, Jack, a successful, self-employed construction developer, felt he had nothing to live for but his work. But Kim resented the fact that his work was his top priority. Kim was refusing to have sex with Jack. Through tears she said, "How can I make love to him when he doesn't even care about me? He almost never takes me out on a date or sits beside me just to talk with me. The only thing he cares about is his work."

Jack's side of the story was altogether different (which is usually the case). He couldn't talk with Kim because she always challenged him. He said he'd given a lot of thought to taking her out on dates. But he knew how she attacked his decisions, and he felt intimidated and afraid that she would attack him even more if they were isolated face-to-face in restaurants. In fact, he wasn't even sure she'd accept his invitations to go out. She always had a "better place" in mind, because she always thought her ideas were "better" than his.

As Bill prayed with these two unhappy people, he brought them to a place where they could hear each other's heartfelt disappointments. Kim expressed how hopeless she felt because Jack never seemed to understand her needs or give her his attention. In Kim's eyes, everything seemed more important to Jack than she did.

Jack, with tears in his eyes, told Kim how deeply he hurt because she gave him no respect. He worked hard day after day, but no matter how large a check he brought home, it was never enough to make her glad or proud of him.

As they listened to each other, Bill watched two people change and soften. Underneath all the pain, both had buried the truth that they cared deeply about each other. Neither had set out to bring grief to the other.

Bill was able to share the Marriage Plus biblical principles of healing, explaining that if each waited for the other to change, they would wait a lifetime. It was essential for both to allow the Lord to release them from their selfishness and begin the restoration of their marriage.

Both Jack and Kim began the humble and courageous steps of risking rejection and failure by trying to meet the other's needs—with no return guarantee. Yet Bill also showed them the underlying promise of God's Word: Give, and you will receive (see Luke 6:38).

Without waiting to "feel" Kim's respect, Jack started trying to show her he loved and cared for her. He took her on dates weekly, called her on the telephone just to say "I love you" and let her know how important she was to his life.

At the same time, Kim didn't wait to "feel" Jack's love for her. She started building him up and never tearing him down (see Prov. 12:4). The result of the two of them "working together with Him" (2 Cor. 6:1) was a glorious testimony of a marriage brought out of the ashes of despair.

Because of this one basic difference—wives crave love and husbands crave respect—let me give two suggestions that can bring you into the beautiful marriage Jack and Kim enjoy today.

1. *Patiently and gently express your needs to your spouse at a time when you are both rested and able to hear each other* (see Prov. 25:11).

2. *Start trying to meet your spouse's need for love or respect whether or not he or she has begun meeting your needs* (see Luke 6:38).

"But," you may ask, "what if I've already been following those guidelines, and they haven't worked?"

Here's my question to you: Have you accompanied your actions by fervent prayer, obedience to the written Word of God and faith that God will answer your requests? If you have been following these two guidelines while praying, obeying and believing God, then notice Luke 18:1: "...at all times they ought to pray and not to lose heart." Don't quit short of the goal line. We will "reap [a harvest] if we do not grow weary" (Gal. 6:9).

You may have another question: "What if my husband or wife is unlovable or can't be respected?"

Your spouse may not be lovable or deserve your respect right now. But if you bail out, he or she may never be.

For encouragement read the book of Esther, the story of a woman God brought into a marriage to save (the Jewish race). In a crisis she went in to the king with this amazing attitude: "If I perish, I perish" (Esth. 4:16). Is that your attitude as a husband or wife?

> Do nothing from selfishness or empty conceit, but with humility of mind let each of you regard one another as more important than himself; do not merely look out for your own personal interests, but also for the interests of others. Have this attitude in yourselves which was also in Christ Jesus, who, although He existed in the form of God, did not regard equality with God a thing to be grasped, but emptied Himself, taking the form of a bond-servant (Phil. 2:3-7).

Are you willing to obey God and serve your undeserving spouse?

Difference 3:
Enjoying the Process vs. Accomplishing the Goal

Yet another typical male-female difference is related to brain function: Women usually enjoy the process of reaching a goal; men usually try to get through all obstacles ASAP to complete the goal.

What woman doesn't love to "stop and smell the roses" along the pathway of her daily schedule? A man? He'll step right on the roses if it can save him three steps to his goal.

Women love to see the scenery on any trip. Men are more apt to go from point A to point B, establishing a new speed record. They enjoy driving like Jehu (see 2 Kin. 9:20). Women may love fine lace tablecloths, while men wouldn't even notice if there was a tablecloth. Women like to browse while shopping; *shopping* is a foreign word to most men. Gary Smalley smiles and says, "Wives shop; husbands hunt!" In other words, wives shop because they enjoy the process; husbands hunt because they want to complete a goal.

Most women are happy taking time to talk, play or make things. They enjoy life less when they get too busy. Most men feel that being busy in the pursuit of "important" goals is far more meaningful than talking, playing or making things. And, of course, they want the sole right of declaring what is or isn't an important goal.

Husbands should notice the reaction both God and the widows had when Dorcas died. Acts 9:39, "...the widows stood beside [Peter] weeping, and showing all the tunics and garments that Dorcas used to make while she was with them." There is many a man who would laugh at these women. But God didn't feel that way. In fact, He immediately gave Peter the power to bring Dorcas back to life!

When I was in Korea in 1973, I had the joy of ministering in a village just outside Seoul. Prior to that time I had always chuckled when I heard of a women's quilting circle, thinking they were probably the church gossips getting together to while away the hours. But in 1973 Korea was hit hard by the worldwide energy crisis. The village church workers were wrapped in quilts, the only thing keeping out the cold. I learned then how vital those quilting circles were. I'm sure the women enjoyed visiting as they stitched, but I no longer saw it as idle time for chatter.

In counseling we often identify communication problems that center on this sex-linked difference. A wife will be trying to share her feelings with her husband. He doesn't really listen, he tries to fix her problem. He wonders why a wife isn't like a car, appliance or other gadget that can be taken apart, tinkered with and fixed. He'll often say, "I could solve all the problems in our marriage if she'd just listen to me."

But a wife doesn't want to be fixed as much as she wants her feelings to be heard. Things may or may not be the way she sees them. That isn't the immediate issue. She wants her husband to catch her vision—right or wrong. A husband needs to let his wife talk, even complain, without interruption and without being told she's wrong. He may not be able to do anything at all about her problem, but if he'll listen and sympathize without argument, his love for her will show through.

What does a wise husband do when his wife is frustrated, angry or emotionally hurting? Care. Find out what she is really saying—not with her words but with her heart. Her words may not express the real source of her pain or worry. Ask questions after she's finished pouring out her heart, living with her "in an understanding way" (1 Pet. 3:7).

Beware: The husband who wants to jump in with answers that seem right to him but not to her may have a wife who believes he is not her answer at all.

There are three things a wise husband must never do: (1) Never tell her she's silly for feeling the way she feels (Prov. 25:20). (2) Never tell her she shouldn't worry about whatever she's upset over (see Eph. 4:29). Praying with her will usually help to end her fears and calm her. (3) Never let her negative response make him negative too (see James 1:19-20).

There's one thing a husband must do: Men desperately need to get in touch with the right sides of their brains and learn to smell the roses— slow down and not feel guilty about it. Hurrying creates more mistakes than victories. Take time to be with your wife and family. The rewards are worth the effort.

If the devil can't get you to sin, his next tactic will be to get you "too busy."

A final word to wives is sufficient: Out of respect for your husband, occasionally and directly seek your husband's problem-solving advice on specific, nonthreatening issues. Watch him smile, knowing he has helped you solve your problem.

To keep your love warm, take time with each other.

THE WORLD NEEDS MORE WARM HEARTS AND FEWER HOT HEADS!

Questions for Reflection and Discussion

1. What attitude does God have toward "unisex"? Study 1 Corinthians 11:11-12; Genesis 2:18; Romans 1:24-32; and 1 Corinthians 6:9-11 before formulating your answer.

2. When you and your spouse were dating, what characteristics did you most admire? Did his or her different ways of doing things, saying things or thinking about things attract you or repel you at first? Have you learned to appreciate those differences, or have they become a stumbling block to you?

3. Both you and your spouse should prepare to answer this question at least a day before you complete the assignment: Without arguing or being defensive, ask your spouse to tell you his or her five deepest needs— needs you could help him or her meet. Listen carefully and write them down. Then reverse roles. For the next month privately pray every day, asking the Lord how to help each of you meet these needs in the other.

4. Again, prepare for this assignment at least a day before you complete it: Working alone, you and your spouse should each make a list of no more than five short-term goals for the two of you to accomplish together within a year. Make a list of no more than five long-term goals to accomplish together within ten years. Share these goals with each other, coming to an agreement on as many as possible. Arrange each set of goals in order of priority. Be sure they are realistic goals which the Lord can bless. Hang them in any attractive place where you will both see them daily. Go over your goals once a month to be certain you are both working toward them. As any goal is accomplished, replace it with a new goal. Memorize Proverbs 29:18.

Dear Ray,

My wife and I have just had the worst vacation of our lives. It was supposed to be a big deal. In a drawing I had won two tickets to Niagara Falls. By the time we flew to New York and got to the falls, I felt like holding her under them. She complained from the minute we started packing until we got home. Nag! Nag! Nag! A complete ten days wasted. Next time I won't let them put my name in for the drawing.

Believe it or not, Ray, we got home and suddenly it was like being with a different woman. She got all sweet and loving. I guess she was just trying to make up for the rotten way she'd acted at the falls. She knew I was really mad. I still am, but things are better now. Who can figure out women anyway? I guess if anybody can, you can. That's why I'm writing. Do women who fly on airplanes get "unnatural," or what was I doing wrong? I don't think I did anything wrong, really, except marry her. If you can explain more about why she acted as she did, clue me in.

Lonely at Niagara

"There is neither...male nor female; for you are all one in Christ Jesus."

Galatians 3:28

FIVE

Women Aren't Men; Men Aren't Women

ALL WEDDINGS ARE HAPPY. IT'S LIVING TOGETHER AFTERWARD THAT CAN CAUSE PROBLEMS!

One of the most ignorant statements a man can utter is, "She's just a woman." Male chauvinism has cost many a man his fortune and family.

Jesus Himself refused to cooperate with anything that smacked of male chauvinism, radically departing from the first-century "party line." The morning prayer quoted by all Jewish men at that time included thanks for not being born "a Gentile, a slave or a woman." Prostitution was rampant in Greek life. Though the Jewish religion frowned on it, it was easy for both Jewish and Greek men to divorce their wives.

But God would have no part of this chauvinism. Jesus Christ had a conversation with a Samaritan woman whose reputation was tainted. No self-respecting rabbi would have talked with her, yet Jesus offered her a transformed, eternal life (see John 4:5-30). He was close friends with Mary and Martha (see Luke 10:38-42). Women even traveled with Christ in ministry (see Luke 8:1-3).

Christ abolishes prejudice. Race, rank and sex are all "one" to Him. The gospel message is and always will be: Give your life to Jesus Christ (see John 14:6; 3:16) and obey God's Word (see John 14:15) in spite of what you have been (see 1 Cor. 6:9-11) and you will find "abundant life" (John 10:10). Our Lord fulfills men *and* women when they really follow Him.

Men can be slow to recognize this truth. After being with and observing Jesus almost daily for more than three years, the apostles wouldn't believe He had risen from the dead because the report the women gave seemed like nonsense to them (see Luke 24:10-11). It's not surprising it was try-a-walk-on-the-water Peter (see Matt. 14:26-32) who took the chance the women were right. Setting aside his own prejudice, he found his Lord risen indeed (see Luke 24:12).

The apostle Paul in Galatians 3:27-29 declared women equal with men in God's eyes, again departing from the blind prejudice of his day. In short, Paul said, "God does not believe men are better than women." Study any other major religion and you will find prejudice, especially toward women. Not so in true Christianity.

Nothing said by Christ or Paul denies the distinctions of womanhood. A woman is not built to be a man. But God's message is that any Christian woman who works at being a woman can stand side by side with *any* man (see Judg. 4:4-23; 2 Chron. 34:22-33; Acts 18:24-26; 2 John 1; et al.).

Some might consider woman being made for man (see Gen. 2:18; 1 Cor. 11:9) a humiliation. But the woman's glory is that she is the only one able to fulfill man (again, see Gen. 2:18). And consider 1 Corinthians 11:11-12: "However, in the Lord, neither is woman independent of man, nor is man independent of woman. For as the woman originates from the man, so also the man has his birth through the woman; and all things originate from God." The Bible eliminates the need for women's lib and replaces it with equal love and caring for both sexes.

Along with the three differences between men and women listed in the last chapter, let's look at four more.

Difference 4:
Intuition vs. Analysis

Some say that women's intuition is a woman's ability to contradict her husband before he says anything!

Seriously, women often have an uncanny sixth sense in which they seem to know something without being told or without exploring or logically analyzing all the facts. I'm not referring to E.S.P. (unless we mean that women are Extra Special People).

A few years ago Harvard University completed a six-year study of seven thousand people of all ages from twenty countries around the world.[1] They concluded that it is "a scientific fact" that "women have greater intuition than men do." Women, even young girls, were found to have a superior ability to judge accurately the feelings and attitudes of other people by merely observing them. Psychologist Judith Hall, who worked on this study, said, "Women are particularly good in the ability to judge negative feelings and mannerisms, or unfriendly feelings, and any signals communicated by the face." She concluded, "There's little doubt women are better than men in nonverbal communication. But we don't know why they have this special ability."

I'll give you the why: God gave this special intuition to women. It is not happenstance that "Wisdom" in the book of Proverbs is female, not male (see Prov. 1:20-21; 2:4; et al.).

Men, don't be surprised if your wife senses what you are feeling before you've said a word—maybe even before you know what you're feeling.

Ladies, in deference to the men, understand why it is hard for them to feel comfortable about women's intuition: Men tend to be analytical. They know what they know by analyzing all the facts with that male logic; they'll make final decisions after looking at all the pros and cons they can unearth. We men are left dumbfounded when our wives know something instantly that we have to learn through painstaking analysis.

Men, listen to your wives and pay attention to their intuition about people, things and opportunities, before you make final decisions.

Even a wife's dreams can be important. If Pontius Pilate had listened to his wife he would have stopped the crucifixion of Jesus Christ (see Matt. 27:19). The ministry I've founded and this book are called Marriage Plus because Arlyne had a dream one night in which God gave her the title.

And yet, intuition can be faulty. How well did intuition serve Eve when she met the serpent? (See Gen. 3:1-6.) Both Bill Gaultiere and I have counseled women who were wrong about their suspicions regarding their husbands. God made husbands to be the spiritual leaders of their homes (see 1 Cor. 11:3) because He knew women might be tempted to rely on their intuition rather than on His Word.

One husband argued: "Intuition is that gift that enables a woman to arrive instantly at an infallible, irrevocable decision without the aid of reason, judgment or discussion." If his definition comes even close to being true, one can see the danger in relying solely on intuition. The Bible is infallible. Intuition isn't. It's as simple as that.

As for male analysis, how well did Adolf Hitler, Charles Manson or Judas Iscariot analyze the truth? If you want the real truth, stick with God's Word (see Ps. 119:96-105).

Difference 5:
Physically Weaker vs. Physically Stronger

You husbands likewise, live with your wives in an understanding way, as with a weaker vessel, since she is a woman; and grant her honor as a fellow heir of the grace of life, so that your prayers may not be hindered (1 Pet. 3:7).

A wife is the physically "weaker vessel" compared to a husband, precisely because she is a woman. In today's society those may sound like fighting words, but give God the benefit of knowing how He designed each part of His creation.

As for the comparative physical strength of women and men, the evidence is conclusive. In many college and professional sports (golf, tennis, basketball, baseball, and so forth) rules are rightly altered—times limited, distances shortened, heights lowered—in order to give less strenuous requirements to women.

As for the comparative physical strength of women and men, the scientific evidence is very conclusive. James Dobson in his powerful book *What Wives Wish Their Husbands Knew About Women* (Tyndale House) wrote:

In functions, woman has several very important ones totally lacking in man—menstruation, pregnancy, lactation. All of these influence her behavior and feelings. She has more different hormones than does man. The same gland behaves differently in two sexes—thus woman's thyroid is larger and more active; it enlarges during pregnancy but also during menstruation...it also contributes to emotional instability—she laughs and cries more easily. Women's blood contains more water (twenty percent fewer red cells). Since these supply oxygen to the body cells, she tires more easily, she's more prone to faint. Her constitutional vitality is, therefore, strictly a long-range matter. When the working day in British factories (under World War II conditions) was increased from ten to twelve hours, accidents among women increased one hundred fifty percent. Of men, not at all.[2]

Someone may say, "Well, women have grown tougher since World War II." But the skyrocketing sickness and death rates of employed women indicate they have not.

None of the above denies women can be—and many are—successful in the work force. The Bible cites examples of gifted, godly women who were employed (see Acts 16:14; 18:2-3; et al.). But the husband who lets his wife wear out because he is not the savior of his wife's body, as Jesus Christ is for His body, the church (see Eph. 5:23), has missed a major part of his God-given assignment as a husband. Paul writes that "If anyone does not provide for his own, and especially for those of his household, he has denied the faith, and is worse than an unbeliever" (1 Tim. 5:8). Neither Paul nor I decided that. God did.

Difference 6:
Depression vs. Inadequacy

Within the body of every healthy woman who hasn't yet reached menopause or had a hysterectomy is a cycle known as ovulation. The vast majority of women complete their menstrual cycles every twenty-eight days. That means fourteen days of hormonal balance and fourteen days of imbalance, which greatly affects their moods. From the time a woman's menstrual period finishes until the egg is released into the Fallopian tubes, her body chemistry is balanced. After the egg is released into the Fallopian tubes her body chemistry is imbalanced. And, oh, what that does to her disposition! In twenty-eight days most women swing from feeling warm and lovable to feeling cold and unlovable.

One day a man comes home and his wife is waiting at the door in her negligee. He scoops her into his arms, carries her into the bedroom and afterward bangs on his chest and says, "It must be this cologne I'm wearing!"

The next day he gets off work early to hurry home for a repeat performance. Only now she's not at the door. When he walks into the kitchen, she isn't there. Finally he spots her huddled in a chair in the living room, crying her eyes out. He walks over to her, reaches out to comfort her, and she turns and snaps, "Don't touch me! All you ever want is sex!" What's happened? Her cycle has changed. If he does touch her, she'll bite him!

Jittery feelings, crying, a hard-to-control temper and deep depression are all common signs during the low points of a woman's month. The good news is she tends to bounce back from her emotional upsets as quickly as she bounced in.

Perhaps the best two things any woman can do to help herself bounce back are to practice James 1:2-4, especially the part about rejoicing when trials come, and to warn her family of her change in cycle: "Please be patient. God's not finished with me yet."

Men, avoid any topic with her during her internal storms that could sink both of your ships! If you see she's not handling the conversation well, back off. Pray for her. Out loud if she'll let you; privately if not.

It is not unusual, for whatever reason, to find women who are uncomfortable at any mention of the menstrual cycle. Those blessed women who have no trouble with their cycles can be especially intolerant of women who do. They tend to think of women who complain about their cycles as cry-babies or cop-outs who make up their sad stories. But 80 percent of women have troubles, some more painful or nerve-wracking than others, with the premenstrual portion of their cycles.

Again, in *What Wives Wish Their Husbands Knew About Women* James Dobson cites behavioral studies of female arrests. In England, France and the United States 49 to 84 percent of women arrested are arrested in the six days before the onset of their menstrual flow. Dobson continues, "Suicides, accidents, a decline in the quality of schoolwork, vision and response speed are all at their worst in the premenstrual period."

A husband needs to be strong and loving even when his wife (or daughter) is depressed and unloving. He needs to let these ladies know that it is all right for them to cry. He needs to assure them that he isn't going to leave them and that he doesn't feel they've failed him by not being strong.

Sex may be out of the question during the blue premenstrual days. Sex in marriage can be wrong when the wife is in an emotionally weak state. At such times she needs to be cuddled and pampered, not made to feel like a sex object. If a wife who is feeling emotionally low receives frequent sexual advances from her insensitive husband, she may develop masochistic, self-destructive ideas. If she starts to believe he only wants her body she may resent her body or her femininity. She may neglect herself physically, losing her motivation to please her husband. She may stop wearing make-up. She may dress sloppily or stop watching her diet. In the midst of this her feelings of failure will increase, creating deeper depression.

Again, ladies, let your husband know when you are emotionally down. When he asks, "What's wrong?" don't say, "Nothing!" Give your reason, but don't try to be too verbal. Just let him hold you.

And men, don't try being "logical" with her at such times. If you are tender and thoughtful with her, she's going to learn to trust you. In fact, she will grow more and more deeply in love with you. Be her man!

One more word to husbands about helping wives: Many men get no more than two consecutive weeks of vacation. And many spend their vacations wondering why they ever married such a cranky, complaining, whining woman. Much of this pain could be eliminated if a husband would keep a monthly calendar and chart out his own wife's menstrual cycle. He could then plan to take her on vacation during the fourteen days she feels at her best.

Of course, many women's cycles are irregular, and a virus or an emotional disturbance can affect any woman's cycle, calling for calendar revisions. Just remember, most women feel at their worst during the six days prior to the onset of their periods. And some women have a few painful days at the beginning of their periods. So the best time for vacations is directly following the wife's period.

A word to tense wives: Although every word in previous paragraphs has been written to bring emotional relief to you who suffer from premenstrual tension, there are some things you can do to reduce your pain.

1. If your problem is severe, it would be wise to get a checkup at a clinic that specializes in releasing women from premenstrual syndrome (PMS). Many women treated in such clinics find quick relief from the tension. A wise, godly doctor can be a real asset.

2. Pray. Jonah, in the stinking belly of a fish, said, "While I was fainting away, I remembered the Lord; and my prayer came to Thee, into Thy holy temple" (Jon. 2:7). Even those who pray only when they are in trouble

know where to turn for help.

3. Praise pays! The Bible doesn't tell us that Paul and Silas had beautiful voices, but it sure does tell us they knew how to sing. They had been physically beaten and thrown in prison, their feet locked in stocks. But that night they sang praises to God, who sent an earthquake to release them from prison. Sing to God (see 1 Cor. 14:15; Ps. 40:1-3). Praise Him. Praise pays!

4. "For though we walk in the flesh, we do not war according to the flesh [yelling at yourself or other people won't help you or them], for the weapons of our warfare are not of the flesh, but divinely powerful for the destruction of fortresses'' (2 Cor. 10:3-4). Put on the whole armor of God (see Eph. 6:10-18) in your imagination, and think about each individual piece as you do it.

"We are destroying speculations and every lofty thing raised up against the knowledge of God, and we are taking every thought captive to the obedience of Christ'' (2 Cor. 10:5). Take all your thoughts captive. Don't let your thoughts take *you* captive.

While a man has no cyclical hormonal imbalances that correspond to a woman's, he often fights feelings of despair and inadequacy. When he doesn't understand what's happening in his wife, he tends to blame himself, which can lead to feelings of failure, which can be destructive to his marriage. Both Ephesians 5:28, "He who loves his own wife loves himself,'' and Ephesians 5:33, "Let each individual among you also love his own wife even as himself,'' show a direct parallel to the truth that a husband will love his wife in proportion to his love for himself. This is why it is so important for a wife to let her husband know that a day's mood is related to her hormones, not something he's done. Each spouse must encourage the other (see Rom. 14:19).

The best thing to do behind a spouse's back is to pat it. In fact, a pat on the back, though only a few vertebrae removed from a kick in the pants, is miles ahead in results!

Difference 7:
Now-Then vs. Now

One curious phenomenon is easy to observe in nearly all men and women. Ask a married man about his honeymoon, and he'll be able to relate a few special memories. Ask his wife about their honeymoon, and she's likely to go on and on and on and on. Why? Because a woman's memory is far more detailed than a man's.

Men tend to think in terms of the present—whatever's happening right now. Women tend to think in terms of the present and the past simultaneously.

Nearly any husband knows that awful feeling of his wife asking, "Do you remember the time when...?" Then she proceeds to describe in vivid detail an experience they shared. She is glowing in her memory of it. And he can't remember it *at all*.

Please realize, wife, that there is a physical reason for his not remembering. It *isn't* that he doesn't care. It *is* that your brains work differently.

There is good news and bad news when it comes to the male memory. The good news is that his forgetter works. He can forgive and forget more easily than his wife. The bad news is that his forgetter often works too well. (How many wives have spent time in tears because their husbands forgot their wedding anniversary?)

The fact is, our brains store memories together with the accompanying emotions. When people have brain surgery under local anesthesia and certain parts of their brains are stimulated, they can recall particular memories *and* the emotions they felt when the remembered event occurred. It's not surprising that women, who tend to have more emotion than men, also have more memories, as either one can trigger the other.

Especially in women, a bad memory (then) can make a bad now.

During my Singles Plus seminars I'm often asked, "Why can't I have sex with the one I love? to We're going to get married!" Then I explain why God cares so much about their avoiding sexual sin: So often an emotionally hurting wife (and sometimes a husband) will say, "I don't like sex with my spouse. Every time, he touches me just as he did before we were married. We had sex then, and we were violating everything we knew to be right in God. I know God says everything is OK now regarding sex between us, but it still feels dirty to me because of what we did *then*."

Thank God for the blood of Christ that cleanses from all repented sin that would otherwise haunt our memories. But we say to every single, as well as every married person, don't create bad "thens"!

I nearly always begin the Marriage Plus seminars by sharing the story of my own marriage, which you've read in earlier chapters. But I usually add another point about the night I surrendered the eighteen-year-old to God and recommitted myself to Him and to my marriage: When I went back to the cabin, woke Arlyne and asked her forgiveness, she forgave me and then left the whole thing with God. By that I mean this: I never told her the details of what went on between the girl and me, and she never asked for details. Both of us followed a pattern set by King David.

After Nathan the prophet had confronted David about his adultery with Bathsheba, David wrote Psalm 51:

> Be gracious to me, O God, according to Thy lovingkindness;
> According to the greatness of Thy compassion blot out my
>   transgressions.
> Wash me thoroughly from my iniquity,
> And cleanse me from my sin.
> For I know my transgressions,
> And my sin is ever before me.
> Against Thee [God], Thee only, I have sinned,
> And done what is evil in Thy sight,
> So that Thou art justified when Thou dost speak,
> And blameless when Thou dost judge (vv. 1-4).

David did the right thing. He didn't blame Bathsheba, as Adam blamed Eve (see Gen. 3:12). Nor did he tell Nathan. Nathan told him (see 2 Sam. 12:1-14). He went to God. God has two abilities we humans do not have. First, God has the ability to forget totally. Second, He has the ability to know exactly what needs to be done to restore a person who repents. God still brought a heavy penalty in David's case (2 Sam. 12:13-14), because He knew David needed it so that he would fully realize the wretchedness of his forgiven sin.

Though humans can forgive, the emotional pain, especially in women, may linger for a long time. The statement "forgive and forget" is nearly impossible for women—and for many men too.

Women have asked both Arlyne and me, "Am I crazy? Six months ago my husband told me about an adulterous affair he'd had. I believe he's repented fully. But I'm still hurting so badly that I cry at the thought of it. It's put a strain on our relationship, especially physically. He keeps saying, 'For the love of Mike, it was a one-time affair, and I told you six whole months ago. Why don't you just forgive and forget?...I have.' ''

We explain to her (and to him, too, if he's present), ''No, you're not crazy. You're just human. Yes, you're a Christian, but you've been terribly violated. It's going to take God's love, a rebuilding of trust and time for you to heal before the pain will subside.''

It was five years before Arlyne could talk about her pain with close friends without crying. By then the pain was past-tense. She explains it beautifully when ministering to women's groups: ''It's like surgery. At first, when you come home from the hospital you don't want anybody brushing up against you. If your little toddler makes a beeline for your lap, you jump up to protect yourself and shout no! But after a while the pain goes away and there's just a scar—a little reminder. It doesn't hurt to have that toddler jump in your lap, just as it doesn't hurt for Ray or me to talk about it today.'' Hallelujah! (And guys, I really had to work hard at rebuilding her trust in me to allow that pain to go away. That took a lot longer than six months.)

God can forget—and does so when we confess our sins to Him and receive His cleansing (see Jer. 31:34). The word *cleanse* in 1 John 1:9 offers total restoration to the Christian life for those who fully repent. Although Arlyne and I still remember what almost sunk our marriage, God has buried our past in the deepest sea and put up a sign saying, No Fishing Allowed! (see Mic. 7:19).

This brings up a big question often asked of us: Should a mate who has been sexually unfaithful tell the spouse after repentance? There is no quick yes or no answer to that question. Some spouses would receive such information as a wound that would be nearly impossible to heal. Many a marriage ends after just such an announcement. Again, the memory is a delicate human instrument, and wives especially feel violated and totally rejected in discovering any infidelity.

Once immorality has been absolutely cleansed by Christ, it may be wise for the guilty partner to carry the emotional pain they will feel without ever telling their spouse what happened or withdrawing from their spouse.

For me it was two years before all my feelings for that young woman left. I have never again communicated with her privately in person or by telephone, never written her a note, never carried her picture and never let my mind dwell on memories, though the devil worked overtime to keep them burning in my mind. Any honest Christian will stop the relationship cold. Otherwise, you violate Ephesians 4:27, "do not give the devil an opportunity."

Some reading this may have had an extramarital affair, then stopped the sexual relationship but continued the friendship. This is most foolish. We as Christians are to "stand firm against the schemes of the devil" (Eph. 6:11), and even then we may well have a "struggle" (v. 12) with "the tempter" (1 Thess. 3:5). I struggled, and the Lord "brought me up out of the pit of destruction" (Ps. 40:2). To grieve over sin is one thing; to *repent* of sin is a bigger step which may require quitting a job, changing churches or even moving to another city. Whatever it requires, it will be worth it. You may still want to argue this point with me. "We can always 'prove' that we are right, but is the Lord convinced?" (Prov. 16:2, LB). "Can a man hold fire against his chest and not be burned?" (Prov. 7:27, LB). You better believe he can't! (And *she* can't either!)

On the other hand, Christian counselors who love Jesus Christ and are committed to using the Bible as their guide for counsel can be very valuable at this point. Rehashing past problems without a wise and godly pastor or counselor who can help you get to the root of the conflict tends to reopen old wounds, not heal them.

James 5:16 tells us, "Therefore, confess your sins to one another, and pray for one another, so that you may be healed." But that disclosure is best done with a counselor whom you both know and trust. That person must know how to help ease the deep pain when one spouse discovers a secret, hidden and causing heartache in the other, who has found the pain too heavy to carry any further.

"The wages of sin is death" (Rom. 6:23). Although adultery, fornication or other sins God condemns do not bring instant death (as eating the fruit didn't bring instant death for Adam and Eve), they have consequences, even after total repentance. The drunk who hits and kills a child does not find the child restored to life because the drunk has sobered up and repented. In just such a way there are repercussions accompanying any sin. The husband who watches his wife cry months or years after his sin has stepped on her heart feels sin's ramifications. And the wife whose husband cries, "How *could* you...?" years after the sin, is reaping some of the wages of sin.

Anyone who thinks God will wink at sexual sin must not be aware of what happened to King David and his kingdom after he failed God with Bathsheba. (Read all about it in 2 Samuel 12:1-14.) Never complain about God being unfair or life being too hard once you've violated God and your spouse. Small wonder Paul tells us to "flee immorality" (1 Cor. 6:18-20). David's adultery nearly cost him his kingdom. Joseph's moral stance in the midst of great temptation (see Gen. 39:10-23) allowed, God in time to make Joseph the second highest leader in Egypt (see Gen. 41:9-45). Do you really want to win—or lose—in life? The winners follow Jesus Christ even when times seem hard. They know where He's headed, and the whole journey is worth the cost (see John 6:68).

There is a heavy sentence for those who do return to being sexually immoral (see 2 Pet. 2). It ain't worth it!

WE ARE PUNISHED FOR OUR SINS
AND ALSO BY THEM!

Questions for Reflection and Discussion

1. Some people claim the Bible is chauvinistic. Read Galatians 3:27-29; Luke 8:1-3; Acts 2:16-17; 18:24-26; 2 John 1, 5; Micah 6:4; Judges 4:4-23; and 2 Chronicles 34:22-33. In light of these passages, what does the Bible say about the superiority of the male gender?

2. Reread the section on the menstrual cycle. Write down all of the suggestions made for women and for men. If you are married, what changes in attitude or actions will make life better for both of you in this regard?

3. Husbands often experience feelings of inadequacy, especially when they can't seem to figure out how to solve family problems. Wives, write out in a list the instructions given you in Ephesians 5:33b (Amplified): "Let the wife see that she respects and reverences her husband—That she notices him, regards him, honors him, prefers him, venerates and esteems him; and that she defers to him, praises him, and loves and admires him exceedingly." After each instruction write at least one practical suggestion to yourself that will help you minimize any feelings of inadequacy in your husband.

4. Are fornication and adultery extremely serious sins? In light of Hebrews 13:4 and Revelation 21:6-8, study 1 Corinthians 6:18-20 and paraphrase these three verses in your own words.

Dear Ray,

A friend told me about your ministry. I'm writing for some help. I am the mother of one child, age four, named Jerry. I love him, and his daddy loves him too. But his daddy now wants me to get a job and put our Jerry in a day-care center.

I am a university graduate. I did well in school, and I know I'm well-qualified for a good-paying job. But here's why I'm writing: I don't want to go to work and leave Jerry. My husband says we need the money, and I'm sure he's right. If I go to work I'm sure I'll be making quite a bit more than he does.

But what can you tell me about day care versus home for a child? Is my four-year-old ready for day care? He seems capable. Maybe I'm just being selfish? A lot of my friends have even younger children in day care. Could you give me some guidelines that would help me make a rational decision or help me with what I can tell my husband?

Thanks.

Real Care About Day Care

*"But if anyone
does not provide for
his own, and especially for those
of his own household, he has
denied the faith, and is worse
than an unbeliever."*

1 Timothy 5:8

SIX

The Mom Bomb

(Only very brave husbands will dare read this chapter!)

THE LATEST THING IN MEN'S
CLOTHING IS WOMEN!

God has called every husband to be his wife's provider. He is responsible for the financial security of the home.

Now 1 Timothy 5:8 is not referring to a man temporarily out of work and honestly searching for a job. Nor is it referring to a man who is sick or handicapped and wisely has his family on welfare. First Timothy 5:8 *is* speaking to the husband who expects his wife to get a job to support him or to "make ends meet." It is referring to the husband who is abandoning his children to whatever or whomever while he forces their mom out of the house to get a job.

"You've Come a Long Way, Baby!"

Adolf Hitler once said, "If you tell a lie often enough it will be believed." And in the late 1960s a big lie started to spread: Two-career families spell success. That lie began because of two reasons: Big business had discovered that women would work for chicken feed compared to what men demanded. Our government (now living on nineteen times the rate of inflation since 1946) suddenly realized homemakers do not pay taxes. So it launched a campaign in cooperation with big business to get the wives and mothers to abandon their homes and become employed. Thus,

Madison Avenue went to work telling women they were just as important as men. (Something the Bible had always said.) Radical women's organizations told women to get out of the house and get a job to prove their worth.

And Americans believed the lie—that two-career families mean more money and a happier home. Although financial collapse is now the number-three reason given for divorce in the United States, money problems aren't solved by selling Mom! In nearly all cases money problems only increase when married mothers find outside employment. In fact, the quick deterioration of our nation's economy and moral fiber is directly related to the mistake of believing this lie.

With a divorce epidemic shattering the stability of the country, latchkey children being abandoned to look after themselves, babies being aborted in the name of convenience and our government being $3 trillion in debt, our nation desperately needs to wake up.

> A man works 'til setting sun,
> A woman's work is never done.

Inside America a bomb is ticking away, louder by the minute. It is the bomb of frustration felt by abandoned wives who have been "sold" on the slave market called the work place. Their God-given calling has been taken away from them in the name of paper money, stamped with the words "In God we trust." Every week I talk to wives who don't want to be where they are—working outside the home. They feel as if they've lost their families; they see no real purpose in their marriages. They ask if I can explain their unhappiness to their husbands. Many of these women feel like failures and hear their husbands saying they *are* failures.

Husbands, wake up! You can revitalize your home life *and* do your part in turning around the national economy.

A Biblical Look at Employed Women

The Bible recognizes godly, professionally successful women. Priscilla was a tent maker along with her husband, Aquila (see Acts 18:2-3). The Bible doesn't mention their having children. Lydia, who sold special cloth, was wealthy enough to own her own home (see Acts 16:14-15). She was a single woman. The "perfect wife" described in Proverbs 31 was gifted in real estate, farming and clothing design.

Some "liberated" women hold the Proverbs wife up as their biblical model for all women because, according to the text, she was employed and had children (see vv. 16, 24, 28). Proverbs 31:16: "She considers a field and buys it; from her earnings she plants a vineyard." She made her own money, and *she controlled it!*

Proverbs 31:24 says: "She makes linen garments and sells them, and supplies belts to the tradesmen." So she was involved in several businesses, each producing a large sum of money.

But it's important to look at the question King Lemuel asks in Proverbs 31:10 (JB), "A perfect wife, who can find?"

The introduction to Proverbs 31 says that King Lemuel's mother taught him this extended poem. Verse 1 reads, "The words of King Lemuel, the oracle which his mother taught him." Traditionally, King Lemuel has been considered a nickname for Solomon, whose mother was Bathsheba. Since Solomon ended up with seven hundred wives and three hundred concubines (see 1 Kin. 11:3), it's obvious he never felt he'd found the perfect wife. He would never find her—no matter how long he looked—because she's a composite picture of many different women.

A New Look at Mother's Day

On nearly every Mother's Day churches all over America hear about "the perfect wife." The guilt of "I don't measure up" sends many a woman home depressed.

The perfect wife is a deeply committed believer (see v. 30), perfection personified (see v. 12), mother-of-the-year (see v. 28), a philanthropist (see v. 20), a gifted real estate investor (see v. 16), a top money manager (see v. 16), a member of the Fortune 500 (see vv. 11, 16), a gourmet cook of foreign foods (see v. 14), farmer-of-the-year (see vv. 16, 18), a disciplined exerciser (see v. 17), totally poised and queenly (see v. 25), a brilliant diplomat (see v. 26), never concerned about her age (see v. 25), in charge of an entire staff at home (see v. 15), a top saleswoman, selling her products over national television (see v. 31) and a fashion designer (see v. 24). She makes an entire wardrobe of winter woolies for her children, husband and staff (see v. 21), always working hard (see v. 27). She never complains (see vv. 12, 26) and never tires (see vv. 15, 18). Her husband sits around chatting with the guys at the gate and never lifts a finger to help her (see v. 23), and she never seems to mind; she just loves him (see v. 12). He's crazy about her too (see vv. 28-29). They have a magnificent marriage and family (see v. 28). Talk about a perfect wife!

Can you see why moms often cringe when they hear about this woman? But what these women usually aren't told is that *no one can live up to her standards.*

Any one woman who tried to do all of the above things would collapse under the weight of the load and *be* in the "above" before her time! And if Proverbs 31 were describing a perfect husband with the same qualifications for a male, no man on earth could live up to him either.

Every woman, even while single, needs to choose prayerfully and carefully which aspects of the Proverbs 31 woman she wants to strive for. God mandates that a woman be a deeply committed Christian believer, which includes being of good character and a good money manager; the rest of this description is a list of optional fine qualities and activities—even marriage itself. With ten million-plus more women than men in the United States (age twenty-five and over), not every woman is going to marry. But since this is a book about marriage, let's look at some considerations of whether or not a wife should be employed.

What Kind of Care Is Day Care?

What does it cost you when someone else raises your children? What is the dollars and cents cost if you abdicate the most important assignment given to parents by God—that of raising your children in the Lord?

Proverbs 22:6 says: "Train up a child in the way he [or she] should go, even when he is old he will not depart from it." By the time a child reaches the age of seven, 80 percent of his or her basic personality and character will be formed and determined—by the TV watched, by the stories and conversations heard and by the role models observed. Who are these role models if Mom is working outside the home? The obvious answer is the day-care providers, and studies are now showing that the kids are coming out on the short end of the stick.

For years articles have claimed that little evidence supported the notion that children of employed mothers are deprived. A study by Dr. Elizabeth Keister in 1970 even suggested that kids in day care were slightly ahead of peers reared solely by their mothers. Other studies in the 1970s showed that the kids in day care might be better socialized and adjust better to full-time school than children brought up at home.

It's taken a few years, but many experts have reversed their attitudes.[1]

In 1987 child psychologist Jay Belsky, one of the early contenders that day care did not adversely affect the development of children, began to express concern over a "slow steady trickle" of evidence that contradicts his earlier view. Belsky concludes that the new studies show two worrisome trends:

First, infants cared for by anyone other than their mothers are more likely to develop insecure relationships to their parents. Apparently infants interpret the daily separations from their mothers as rejection; it seems that, to protect themselves from this trauma, they withdraw emotionally from their mothers. In Michigan one study of one-year-olds found that children in full-time day care exhibited greater avoidance of their mothers than did parent-reared children.

Second, children with a record of early nonparental care not only are not ahead of their peers, but the evidence shows psychological harm. At the University of North Carolina a study of five- to eight-year-olds who had spent most of their early years in a highly regarded day care center showed more tendencies to hit, kick, threaten and argue than those who had not been in day care or who had started after the age of three. If you've ever observed a group of two-year-olds interact, you begin to understand the concept of survival of the fittest!

Another study of children from middle-class families in the Dallas area showed that by the third grade those who had spent extensive time in child-care centers were more uncooperative and less popular and had poorer grades and study skills and less self-esteem than children cared for at home.

I can't put a dollar figure on these problems, though our society is paying a dangerously high price for Mom working outside the home. What I *can* put a price on is how much it costs both Dad and Mom, as well as little Timmy, in dollars and cents.

Does It Pay for a Mother to Be Employed?

In 1948 18 percent of mothers were employed outside the home. In 1990 this figure is more than 70 percent. One government study projects this will rise to more than 80 percent by the year 2000.

In this age of ego enhancement you might think most mothers take jobs outside the home to be "fulfilled." But at the University of Michigan a study updated frequently shows that over half of all mothers enter the job force to help take care of present needs. Their secondary reason is to fund future needs—retirement or housing. Most mothers work because it seems the family cannot make it without two incomes. Are they right?

We'll consider this question from several angles; let's first look at the financial picture by looking at a hypothetical family.

We'll say a father has a full-time job earning $25,000 per year. He and his wife have two children, one being a preschooler who needs full-time day care if Mother is employed—which she is. The wage Mom makes will vary from city to city and depend on her education and job skills. In most cities the wage will range from between $5 to $10 an hour. So let's say she makes $10 an hour, $400 a week.

What financial obligations will an employed wife have?

My good friend and adviser Malcolm MacGregor, author of *Your Money Matters*, conducts Money Matters Seminars all over the world. Marshall and Bea Berman have been my longtime friends and ministry accountants for many years. These three have worked with me to give you the high cost of a "mom bomb," as presented here:

1. *Taxes:* As a certified public accountant, Malcolm has analyzed the tax burden at many income levels. Though there are too many variables— the husband's salary, child-care credits, state income tax and so forth—to give exact figures, using the 1990 tax rates Malcolm estimates that when a husband earns $25,000 the government takes 25 percent of a wife's $20,800 income. For each $2,000 added to the wife's income, add 1 percent until you reach $30,000 (that is, 31 percent at $30,000), and then 1 percent for each additional $1,000 up to $40,000. At $400 per week, we'll estimate the tax burden at 25 percent, or $140 per week. (If there are state taxes where this couple lives, the taxes will be much higher.)

2. *Transportation:* This expense is more than the extra $20 a week spent on gasoline. It is also the extra wear and tear on the car, higher insurance rates, shorter vehicle lifespan and so forth. Using Hertz Corporation[2] figures, a compact car purchased when it is four years old and driven for five years will cost thirty-one to forty-six cents per mile to operate.

If Mom drives an extra twenty miles each day, taking the kids to the day-care center, going to work and reversing the route to get home, the extra one hundred miles a week will cost between $31 and $46. Let's say $38. Any car larger than a compact will cost much more.

3. *Tithes:* If this $40 isn't given to God, Satan will steal it. People who don't tithe are financial losers, continually asking, "Where does all the money go?" (see Mal. 3:8-12; 2:2; Hag. 1:2-10; Luke 11:42; Heb. 7:4-6; et al.). Any financial success that lasts requires tithing and generous giving above the tithe. God says, "Test me now in this" (Mal. 3:10).

4. *Food:* If Mom is employed, food costs are likely to increase in three areas. Lunch: Mom is already eating lunch, but most employed mothers don't pack a sandwich but buy their lunches out. Then there's the coffee and snacks at breaks and any costs of company coffee clubs, etc. Six dollars a day is a conservative minimum for our mom. It adds up—$30 a week.

Dinner out: If you've got enough dough you can have pizza. When both Mom and Dad work outside the home they eat out significantly more often (one study suggests almost three-and-a-half times more often) than when Mom is not employed. More than half of all meals eaten in America are eaten away from home. Many schools now offer both breakfast and lunch programs, and the drive-up windows of fast-food restaurants always seem crowded.

In 1970 when I visited Gresham, Oregon, there was just one restaurant on the road to the Mount Hood ski areas. Today more than forty restaurants line a one-mile strip, jokingly referred to as "The Maalox Mile." You can see this huge increase in food handlers in almost any American community. When you couple eating out with the increased reliance on take-out and delivery food, it isn't difficult for our family of four to increase their food expense by $40 a week.

Lost bargains: This shopping expense is a wipeout for the family because Mom has no time to comparison shop, make food from scratch, knit and sew and the like. Though I've listed this under the category of food, it is somewhat broader in scope. By not shopping well, by buying prepackaged or machine-made products, Mom can eat up 8 to 14 percent of her income, depending on where she lives. Let's take the lowest figure—8 percent—which translates into $32 per week.

5. *Personal care:* The most obvious item to be considered in this category

is clothing. Working in an office, a woman can go through $10 a week in hosiery alone.

If Mom is involved in a competitive job, that is, if she is moving up in management, she will have to dress better than her male competition. I'm not saying this is fair; it's just an unfortunate reality. A "power" wardrobe will easily cost $2,500 a year and more.

At the other end of the spectrum is a job that requires the purchase of a few uniforms and special shoes at $250 a year. I'm going to pick a conservative lower-end figure of $30 per week. (Many women will note how ridiculously low that figure is. In many occupations a woman who wore a wardrobe costing $1,000 a year "couldn't be seen in public.")

The second personal care cost would cover extra cosmetics, beauty care and hair maintenance. The employed mother tends to go to the beauty parlor more often than when she was not getting a personal paycheck. After all, she needs to be well-groomed to receive the compliments she seldom gets at home.

Since we assume that Mom is already having her hair cut from time to time and already uses personal care and beauty products, we're going to allow a small marginal increase of $10 per week.

The final personal expense is "I owe it to myself" and a parallel guilt offering. Mom, you do owe it to yourself. You are holding down three full-time jobs: mother, homemaker and outside slave for hire! The emotional drain of knowing you're constantly exhausting yourself and doing what you hate means you *do* deserve a break today.

You'll wake up late one morning, break something in your rush, have short words with your hubby, get a speeding ticket on the way to the child-care center and arrive late to work for the first time in two years—to find that this is one of the rare mornings when your boss beats you in! At lunchtime you walk by a sidewalk sale and see a $99.95 outfit on sale for $39.95. You really can't afford $40, but you try it on anyway. It fits perfectly. You buy it with a shrug and say, "I owe it to myself." If you have already budgeted just $10 a week for this category, you've just gone through four weeks' allotment.

Then there's the guilt offering expense. You wake up at 6 A.M. to discover that Timmy has a fever. You can't take him to the regular day-care center (unless you are in a city with a special center for children with contagious illnesses—at $50 a day), but, fortunately, your sister can take care of him. All day long you're haunted by his good-bye: his outstretched hands and his sobbing "Mommmmyyyy!" You'll bring Timmy a new toy that evening. Right? This leads to the very obvious next expense.

6. *Child care:* We face a real child-care crisis. Some families are fortunate because they have a Christ-centered relative or close family friend willing to watch the children at little or no cost. But national statistics show that child-care costs are 23 to 40 percent of the wife's income. Using the midpoint of 32 percent, our mother would spend $128 per week (32 percent of the wife's income of $400 per week). This figure, however, would be low if she has a child under five in a full-time day-care center and one in day care after school.

7. *Job expense:* This final expense of $4 a week might cover union dues or office expenses, such as a "kitty" to buy flowers and gifts, tickets to help co-workers' kids earn money to go to camp, Little League candy, Girl Scout cookies, etc.

Are there other expenses? You bet! How about extra medical costs? Kids in day care are exposed to every germ and become ill more often. This may be covered by insurance, but if Mom has to stay home with a child, she doesn't get paid and there is a lost day's wage. The stress level is high among employed mothers because of the pressures, and this too can lead to extra medical expense and sick days, possibly unpaid.

What about a job that requires a wardrobe that needs extensive dry-cleaning? This can amount to $20 to $25 per week.

What happens if Mom can't get to the day-care center by 6 P.M.—due to traffic problems, emergency overtime, car breakdowns, etc.? Most centers charge a penalty if a parent is more than five minutes late. One center charges $50 if you're more than twenty minutes late.

To relieve the work load, Mom might hire a cleaning lady several times a month. Many cities now have grocery shopping services.

What happens when the car Mom drives to work gives out? How is she going to program into her budget a $230-a-month car payment?

We could continue to count costs, but let's just summarize money spent up to this point:

Taxes	$140	
Transportation	38	
Tithe	40	
Lunch	30	
Eating out/take-out food	40	
Lost savings	32	
Clothes	30	
Personal care	10	
I owe it to myself/guilt	10	
Child care	128	
Employment expenses	4	
Total	$502	weekly
Wages	$400	weekly
Total loss	$102	weekly

It is a rare wife and family that can stick to these conservative figures, which assume not one single unexpected problem. (And if you say you've beaten this system, how much do you owe right now on credit cards and unpaid bills? How long can you keep this up?)

Someone reading this who makes $400 a week is saying, "But I don't have a preschool child. My only son, or daughter, is ten." Yet after-school care for a child under twelve will cost $30 to $50 a week.

Some husband is saying, "Aha! Gotcha there, Ray! Our only child, an eleven-year-old, stays with his Aunt Gertrude after school. She's a Christian and charges us nothing." Or, "Ha! Ha! My wife and I don't have *any* children and don't plan to have any children. So with both of us in the work force we can make a bundle."

But a wife working outside the home puts a strain on a marital relationship. The statistics are in: Even without children, higher incomes mean higher risk of divorce. Is it any surprise the divorce epidemic is so high when both spouses are exhausted? Instead of shouting for joy, they shout at each other.

Should your wife be employed outside your home?

I'm not saying every wife and mother must stay at home, though she should never let others take the responsibility for raising her children. Some women can be employed and raise their children well. Many schoolteachers, for example, have done so for several generations. But there is a great and vital difference between women who love their work, love their families and somehow manage both, and women who don't or can't. Careful consideration needs to be given to determine if a wife should be employed outside the home.

1. Husband, first examine your own heart, asking yourself, "Do I want my wife to be employed?" If the answer is yes, the second question is "Why?" First Timothy 5:8 says that you as a husband are to be the provider for your family's needs. Is she going to take over and usurp your assignment from the Lord?

2. Husband, are you forcing your wife to be employed? Before marriage the average guy worries what would happen to his bride if he lost his job. After marriage he wonders what would happen to *him* if she lost *her* job! But 1 Peter 3:7 and Ephesians 5:23, among other verses, tell you, husband, to be the "savior" of your wife's body. Certainly no "savior" would thrust his wife into overwork. If you are reading this book you must want God's real answers, which include real answers for your wife as well as you. She should work away from home only by choice—not because you've driven her into it.

Before any child arrives, the wife may want to be employed. If both spouses agree that this is a good idea and they can financially afford it, it may work fine. Fine, that is, if the wife holds her job lightly, being willing to let it go at any time, and if the couple doesn't make the common mistake of creating the false security of a double salary. But if her salary has been added to his to pay expensive, long-term debts (mortgage, car, etc.), when a baby arrives and the wife stays home this couple will suddenly discover themselves in a bind: two salaries cut to one with three mouths to feed. So the wife's salary should be used only for extra items that will improve the home or their lives, investments or offerings to God, which will increase the family income (see Luke 6:38). No wife should ever be employed to "make ends meet."

3. Does your wife really want to work away from home? If the answer is yes, the next question is "Why?" Is it to fulfill a basic need in her? Or is it to escape? Wanting employment outside the home is wrong if she's doing it because she feels inferior because she is "just" a housewife.

Girls today are reared with full expectations that they'll enter into a career. Moms and dads are eager to see their daughters graduate from universities and get degrees. They're proud to see their daughters get good jobs with opportunities for promotion.

Then along comes marriage and her career suddenly gets replaced by routine housework and soon stacks of dirty diapers. The baby cries; the husband watches TV while the wife washes pots and pans. She starts to wonder if she really wants to spend the rest of her life this way.

She hears women's lib shout, "Leave those pots and pans. Get out of the house and get a job!" On television she sees half-hour comedies and dramas that show women successfully juggling a family and a full career. Don't the programs imply that she's stupid if she doesn't get out there and do it too?

One such program is about a single mother who, on the sly, goes out and breaks up spy rings, risking her life. With the help of their single grandmother the kids get along just fine. They never notice when she's gone, and she's never tired when she's home. Right before your eyes—talk about adventure! Any woman can do that, can't she? Some women and a lot of husbands think so.

Of course, creative human beings—male or female—need to express their gifts. They need to feel their work is appreciated and of value. But escape isn't the answer. Acting upon God's Word is the answer.

Unless the husband wakes up to his role, as God has designed it, and meets her needs, the wife is bound to feel trapped. The one who makes the pivotal difference in a wife's attitude about almost everything is the husband. If he lets her know he treasures her and isn't just using her or taking her for granted, she is likely to be satisfied working at home.

4. How much energy does your wife have? Is she a ball of fire at midnight? Or is she pooped out by the time you get home from work? Worn out wives are rarely much fun to be around. They can't be everything God designed them to be. If she expends all her energy on an outside job, there's none left for you or the children. Instead of the wife enjoying those cute things the kids do because they're kids, she yells, screams or slaps because she's too tired to appreciate them—or you.

5. How well is she allocating her time? Does your wife have her responsibilities scheduled in unhassled time slots so that her work doesn't stack

up? A wife who has too much work left undone at the end of the day is almost always going to let you know—loudly. She'll either yell at you or at things in general. Her frustrations will soon become your frustrations.

6. What's your honest attitude, husband, about doing housework? Cooking the meals? Making the beds? Doing the dishes? I wish I had a special eraser that could erase one phrase out of every human mouth—*the working wife*—used to describe only the employed wife. Men, haven't you noticed? *All wives work!* Wives work whether or not they are paid for it, and they work hard. They have full-time jobs inside the home. Housework requires approximately thirty hours every week, and that is with no special occasions to prepare for. Do you feel you have an equal responsibility with your wife to do this housework? If she has, in your opinion, an equal responsibility to work *outside* the home, then it only stands to reason that you have an equal responsibility to work inside the home.

Think it's time for you to retire and take it easy? Every retired husband is responsible for a maid or for half the housework. Otherwise, a retired husband is simply a wife's full-time job!

7. God gave you children to raise. What are you going to tell Jesus Christ if you and your wife don't raise them?

The most difficult thing to replace is a mother who isn't home. Whether you are saved or lost, Romans 14:12 promises there will come a time when you will have to face Jesus Christ. I guarantee that He is not going to ask, "How was business?" You can be sure He will ask, "How well did you raise those children I gave you?" I pray you'll have a good answer.

Someone has said, "The hand that rocks the cradle today charges $5 an hour." But the truth is: "The hand that rocks the cradle rules the world." Are you willing to trust your kids to surrogate parents?

8. Who will be with your children if a parent isn't home when they get home from school? More than ten million American children and teenagers come home daily to an empty house or apartment. America's future is growing up with no real love and discipline. It's growing up with an influential role model: color TV. What are your children and teenagers watching when you aren't home that may affect their entire lives?

Children and teenagers need the security of someone to talk to after school. If a parent isn't home, children are likely to go looking for someone else to talk to—and the company they keep may not be the company you like. The devil comes because the house is empty (see Matt. 12:43-45). Who's talking to them? Who's influencing them if Mom and Dad aren't home? Be sure you know the full answer to that question.

It's not enough to teach children about the 911 emergency number. Do teach them that whether Mom is home or not. But "what will a man be profited, if he gains the whole world, and forfeits his soul?" (Matt. 16:26). More to the point, what would it profit you if you lost your own son or daughter's soul? Would you sell your child's soul to the devil for a million dollars? But are you selling your child's soul for *two salaries?*

9. If she is the provider, what good are you to her? Vassar economist Shirley Johnson has calculated that for every thousand dollars a year a wife earns, her chances for divorce increase by 2 percent.

The divorce rate of high-salaried women is more than twice the average of all women, and for women executives earning $50,000 or more it's four times the national average.

10. Will temptation draw her away from you? Adultery and divorce are rampant among employed wives. A right-brained woman is looking for a relationship with you—or with someone. That someone could be a file clerk who pays attention to her. Or, if she spends more time with the boss than she does with you, she may become emotionally attracted to the boss. That happens often.

God's Provision for Your Needs

If you are panicked because you feel you can't make ends meet without two paychecks, read on. In every Marriage Plus seminar I spend two hours teaching on "God's Plan for Abundant Finance." I'm well aware that "prosperity teaching" can get out of line. Some of it deserves to be mocked, as it is. But more than a thousand times in the Bible God says He *wants* His people to prosper—as a blessing and as a means to reach the world with His Good News (see 2 Cor. 9:8). Christ died for every person (see 2 Pet. 3:9). It may sound crass, but it takes great sums of money to take the gospel to every human being, giving each the opportunity to accept or reject the Lord, and then teach them the ways of the Lord. God makes Christians "prosperous" if He knows He can fully trust them to use large portions of their money to continue spreading His Word. I do not have room to share here all the Bible says about God's plan, but I will focus briefly on the following verses:

Psalm 35:27: "Let them shout for joy and rejoice, who favor my vindication; and let them say continually, 'The Lord be magnified, who delights in the prosperity of His servant.' "

Proverbs 15:6: "Much wealth is in the house of the righteous, but trouble is in the income of the wicked."

Proverbs 22:4 (Amplified): "The reward of humility and the reverent and worshipful fear of the Lord is riches and honor and life."

Psalm 34:10: "...they who seek the Lord shall not be in want of any good thing."

Romans 10:12: "For there is no distinction between Jew and Greek; for the same Lord is Lord of all, abounding in riches for all who call upon Him."

First Timothy 6:17: "[Don't] fix [your] hope on the uncertainty of riches, but on God, who richly supplies us with all things to enjoy."

Galatians 3:29 says, "And if you belong to Christ, then you are Abraham's offspring, heirs according to promise." Abraham was a wealthy man. We are his heirs. He was given his riches by God so that God could carry out His plan to bless all nations (see Gal. 3:8). Ultimately the blessing would come through the birth of Jesus Christ (see Matt. 1:1). But the *Living Bible* rightly says, "...all of God's promises to [Abraham] belong to us" (Gal. 3:29). God's whole New Testament concept of tithing (see Heb. 7:1-3; Gen. 14:17-20) and giving so that you will receive (see Luke 6:38; 2 Cor. 9:6-12) is totally tied up in this truth.

When it comes to finance, no verse in Scripture carries more promise for Christians than 2 Corinthians 9:8: "And God is able to make all grace abound to you, that always having all sufficiency in everything, you may have an abundance for every good deed."

Deuteronomy 8:18 will always be true: "But you shall remember the Lord your God, for it is He who is giving you power to make wealth, that He may confirm His covenant which He swore to your fathers, as it is this day."

If you really believe God is the One who is "giving you power to make wealth," why are you as husband and wife so eager for *both* of you to go out and get jobs? Is "In God we trust" true for your household?

Remember, God has the ability to bless your finances or allow them to disappear (see Mal. 3:10-12). It all depends on whether you trust and obey Him, acting upon His word.

Matthew 6:31 says, "Do not be anxious then, saying, 'What shall we eat?' or 'What shall we drink?' or ⁰With what shall we clothe ourselves?' " Since you've known Jesus Christ, has there been a moment when you asked, "How are we going to afford to buy food with the prices going up the way they are?" Or, "How on earth am I going to buy any new clothes?" Can you see that such talk is absolutely forbidden by the Lord? That kind of talk comes from a fear that Jesus Christ doesn't really love you as an individual or care what happens to you.

Jesus Christ continues in Matthew 6:32-33, "For all these things the Gentiles [all people who don't know the Lord] eagerly seek; for your heavenly Father knows that you need all these things. But seek first His kingdom and His righteousness; and all these things shall be added to you."

None of the above is intended by God to be a get-rich-quick scheme. In Proverbs 30:7-9 Agur prays as we all should be praying:

> O God, I beg two favors from you before I die: First, help me never to tell a lie. Second, give me neither poverty nor riches! Give me just enough to satisfy my needs! For if I grow rich, I may become content without God. And if I am too poor, I may steal, and thus insult God's holy name (LB).

Is Agur's prayer your prayer? If not, you are probably caught up in this world's wheeling-dealing "prosperity," which is likely to end in a crash: "Like a bird that fills her nest with young she has not hatched and which will soon desert her and fly away, so is the man who gets his wealth by unjust means. Sooner or later he will lose his riches and at the end of his life become a poor old fool" (Jer. 17:11, LB).

As for Me and My House

Gary Amos, associate professor of law and government at Regent University (CBN) in Virginia Beach, Virginia, teaches family law. His recent book, *Defending the Declaration*, has been cited in a brief to the United States Supreme Court. Amos wrote:

God does not give anyone the freedom to make the kinds of choices and decisions that hurt the family. He does not give anyone the right to do wrong. The family structure is the first place where God intends for us to practice responsible self-government....He specifically commands (each) father to teach his children (Eph. 6:4)....When we throw away love and a sense of duty, we begin to expect others to shoulder our responsibilities. That is why our families are no longer a system of welfare, but have become the objects of welfare. We no longer teach our children thrift and fiscal responsibility at home because all of our economic activities are carried on outside the home. We've stopped teaching our children at home, within the family, which is their normal social context....We do not take time to love our children and meet their emotional needs. Instead, whenever problems arise we send them to "experts." We alienate our children and leave them to themselves. Why should we be surprised that they are too busy for us when we get old and helpless? Why shouldn't we spend our final days in a rest home, lonely and alone, longing for a visit from our children whom we hardly knew?[3]

Consider two men, close relatives who knew God. One was Abraham. The other was Lot. Notice what God said about Abraham: "For I know him, I know he will command his children and his household, too, and they will keep the way of the Lord, and will be fair and make good decisions, so that I, the Lord, can fulfill my promises to Abraham" (Gen. 18:19, KJV). God was saying, "Abraham is a man I can trust. I know him. When the chips are down, ultimately, he will obey me." God made Abraham "father of a multitude of nations" (Gen. 17:4).

Now look at Abraham's fumbling nephew, Lot: "And Lot went out and spoke to his sons-in-law, who were to marry his daughters, and said, 'Up, get out of this place, for the Lord will destroy the city.' But he appeared to his sons-in-law to be jesting" (Gen. 19:14). They didn't take Lot seriously. "But his wife, from behind him, looked back [disobeying God, see verse 17]; and she became a pillar of salt" (Gen. 19:26).

Ask yourself right now: Which kind of father am I to my family? Am I like Abraham? Or like Lot?

Ask yourself right now: Which kind of wife am I to my husband? Am

I like Sarah (see 1 Pet. 3:6)? Or am I like Lot's wife?

The results of each home speak for themselves. If you're like Lot or his wife, it's time to change your ways.

All marriages go through various kinds of "storms" (see Matt. 7:24-27), some of which are economic. But before the days when some husbands began thinking their wives should be shoved out of their homes to "make ends meet," or wives began to demand so-called economic freedom, the Christian couple was forced to tough it out and trust God's Word. They learned to pray. They tithed the husband's income and gave above their tithe. They paid their bills. When things were tight they learned to be economical. When things got better they even took vacations. Because they followed God's financial directions, the couple was thrilled to discover God keeps His Word. He proved His Word over and over again as He fed, clothed and sheltered them (see Matt. 6:31-33).

From time to time the husband got raises at work, and the family income continued to improve. The husband kept the respect of his wife because he was the provider. The children grew up with the security of knowing their mom and dad as parents in their home. By what they observed from parental role models, they learned that they had a friend in Jesus (see Deut. 6:6-7; Eph. 6:4). There was a loving bond established among them all. Even when Dad was tired, he was respected because everyone knew he was working hard to bless his wife and family. In short, they had a Christian home.

LOTS OF PEOPLE WHO LOOKED TO GOD TO SAVE THEM NOW EXPECT THE GOVERNMENT TO DO IT. IT WON'T!

"For what will a man be profited, if he gains the whole world, and forfeits his soul? Or what will a man give in exchange for his soul?" (Matt. 16:26).

IN YOUR QUEST FOR RICHES, DON'T LOSE
THE THINGS THAT MONEY CAN'T BUY!

Questions for Reflection and Discussion

1. As a wife, or as a single woman, reread the description of the Proverbs 31 "perfect wife." Remember this description is not of one woman, but is a composite picture of many women. Which aspects of this woman do you have now? Which of the four attributes she possesses do you see as goals for your life?

2. Spend four hours watching prime-time television programs. Write down a description of the portrayal of every employed wife you see. Does she seem full of vitality and able to cope with all pressures? How realistic is this? Do the same thing with all commercials that show an employed wife. Write a paragraph expressing your own feelings about how honest these portrayals have been and how important the influence of television is on "selling America" on the employed wife.

3. If you are an employed wife, reread the financial expense categories listed in this chapter. Write down what it costs you to be employed. What is your financial net gain or loss? Discuss this figure with your spouse.

4. If you are an employed wife, list what it costs you spiritually and physically to be employed. To you and each member of your family, what is the net gain or loss of your employment?

5. Read Matthew 6:31-33; Deuteronomy 8:18; Malachi 3:8-18; Matthew 23:23; Luke 11:42; 2 Thessalonians 3:10-12; and 2 Corinthians 9:6-12. What is God's promise to you if you act upon His Word? Write that promise down by paraphrasing 2 Corinthians 9:6-12.

Dear Ray,

I'm a new Christian and so is my wife. We're trying to do everything just right. But our pastor says I'm head of the house, and my wife isn't happy about that. When I even make a suggestion she's always got a "better" one. What bothers me is, sometimes she's right. Then I feel stupid because I'm the one who's supposed to be calling the shots. I know you teach on husbands and wives in your seminar. I haven't been to one of them yet. We plan to get to one, but I need some quick help now. Could you explain what being head of the house really means?

The Boss

"Husbands, love your wives, just as Christ also loved the church and gave Himself up for her."

Ephesians 5:25

SEVEN

The Husband
Who Uses His Head

WANTED

A good woman who can clean and cook fish, dig worms, sew and owns a fishing boat and motor. Please enclose photo of boat and motor.

The above sign is meant to be funny. But too many wives married to fishermen don't see it that way. They believe their husbands are more interested in fishing than in them. And you don't have to be a fisherman's wife to feel like a barnacle on your husband's ship of life. The golfer's wife can find him putting golf balls instead of puttering with her. The politician's wife can feel she's married to just one long filibuster. God never intended things to be this way.

It's my prayer that you will soon be able to join me for a Marriage Plus seminar. So many miracles happen at the live seminars. (Oh, and when you come, wear loose clothing, as you're going to be laughing a lot!)

God has never intended you to think His directions for marriage are just good suggestions or high ideals. They can be lived. Acting upon God's Word remains the one key to a great marriage.

In an excellent cassette tape series called "One Flesh," a biblical study of marriage, Pastor Bob Yandian of Grace Fellowship in Tulsa, Oklahoma, makes a right-on comment about the first wife being made from a rib (see Gen. 2:21-22). He says, "*Rib,* in the Hebrew language, nearly always refers to a literal rib. But in 1 Kings 7:3 the Bible accurately translates it *beams,* referring to the beams or pillars that held up Solomon's house." He continues, "You husbands may seem outstanding to everyone. But your wife is the beam that holds you up. She's the hidden, inward support. Without her you'd fall apart.''

The Covenant of Marriage

Marriage is the forming of a covenant relationship between a single male and female. As Keith Intrater says in his book *Covenant Relationships* (Destiny Image Publishers), ''...the purpose of a covenant is to guarantee a given relationship. The covenant itself is actually a set of words that are spoken to define the nature of that relationship and set forth the principles of commitment to it....The covenant of marriage is the words of oath commitment that pass between [a marrying couple] at the marriage ceremony and seal them forever.''

Malachi 2:16 says that God "hates divorce." He knows the destruction it brings (spiritually, emotionally and often physically) to the people He loves. But nowhere does God say that He hates divorced people. Yet He clearly says that heavy penalties (see Rom. 1:27) will be paid (here or in eternity) for "covenant breakers" (Rom. 1:31, KJV).

Husbands and wives who loosely handle their wedding covenant will have ineffective prayer lives (Mark 11:23-26; 1 Pet. 3:7; and others). They ask but do not receive. God was speaking to this issue when He said to a divorced husband or a husband treating his wife badly or contemplating divorce,

> You cover the altar of the Lord with tears, with weeping and with groaning, because He no longer regards the offering or accepts it with favor from your hand. Yet you say, "For what reason?" Because the Lord has been a witness between you and the wife of your youth, against whom you have dealt treacherously, though she is your companion and your wife by covenant. But not one has done so who has a remnant of the Spirit....Take heed then, to your spirit, and let no one deal treacherously against the wife of your youth (Mal. 2:13-15).

In almost every divorce there is the "untrustworthy" (the New American Standard Bible translation of "covenant breakers" in Romans 1:31) partner, who sinfully and callously violates the commitment to the marriage covenant. Often there is also the victim of the divorce, who has given every effort to keep his or her commitment to the covenant. God intends for both partners to keep their covenantal marriage vows. Far more, God intends both spouses to keep their commitments to His design for marriage and Christian family life, as given in the Bible.

Working Together With Christ

Even though a man and woman become one in marriage (see Gen. 2:24), it takes a third party—Jesus Christ—to have a Christian marriage. When one marriage partner fails to honor Christ, the committed spouse "working together" with Christ (2 Cor. 6:1) can bring the wayward spouse into a place of order (see 1 Cor. 7:14; 1 Pet. 3:1-2; Prov. 21:1; 2 Kin. 19:28). The Lord moves mightily for those who pray believing His Word. I meet a staggering number of formerly rebellious husbands and wives who have been miraculously transformed through the power of their Christian spouses' prayer and trust in God.

Let me share another story about Arlyne and her prayer for me and our marriage.

In 1980, after ten years of wholeness in ministry, I went through a horrible midlife crisis. I suffered all of the dreadful symptoms listed by Jim and Sally Conway in their excellent books on the subject. I knew every answer for marriage. I didn't know one for myself! I wanted to run away. My darlin' Arlyne prayed for me and loved me as best she could in such a despairing time. My closest Christian friends prayed too and loved me in Christ. Several talked very honestly with me about my need to be made whole again and to surrender to the Lord.

One day, while on vacation with friends nine months after my midlife crisis began (the friends were away at the moment), I was shouting at Arlyne and said, "I think I still want a divorce!" I, in fact, had said that several times during the preceding months. This time she looked at me and said, "OK, if you're going to leave me, leave now! At least our friends will help me get through this. God is my defense."

I was stunned. I knew she meant what she'd said. I had the option of walking out on my marriage, my kids, my ministry—everything the Lord had done in my life. Suddenly I had a glimpse of how I'd been walking away from Christ in the past nine months. But reality sometimes seeps in slowly.

A few minutes later, in all my cockiness, I strode into the bedroom where Arlyne had retreated to pray. I began yelling at her all over again. But I stopped in midsentence. I thought, Why am I yelling at her like this? She hasn't done anything wrong. It's *me;* I'm out of step!

Then and there I was "delivered" from the midlife crisis. I broke into tears and sobbed for a long time. "Godly grief produces a repentance that leads to salvation" (2 Cor. 7:10). The Greek word for *salvation* is *sozo,* which often refers to deliverance. Whatever your understanding of deliverance is, I was that day delivered forever from many tormenting spirits that had haunted me since my early teen years. Thank God for my darlin' Arlyne, a praying wife who would not stand by idly and watch me fall away.

I know James Dobson has taken some heat for writing *Love Must Be Tough* (Word), but I highly recommend that book everywhere I go. It is a book that beautifully describes "speaking the truth in love" (Eph. 4:15). When one sinning spouse causes spiritual, emotional or physical damage to children, teenagers or the other spouse, that sin must be confronted. *Love Must Be Tough* tells the spouse who must do the confronting *how* to do it in God's love. Any spouse whose mate is deeply committed to sin should read that book and follow Dobson's directions.

Rebellious humans still have free will. Sometimes when a sinful, callous marriage partner willfully violates the covenant commitment, divorce becomes inevitable. When this happens, the covenant-breaker is in deep trouble with God. This is not the case for the spouse who has done all he or she can to follow God's directions to restore the covenant and has been waging spiritual warfare (see Eph. 6:10-18), waiting and believing the Lord on behalf of the fallen spouse. Our God is a merciful and loving Father who will uphold the faithful, yet violated, marriage partner (see Heb. 13:5b).

God's Word Stands

Marriage is God's idea. That's why it's under so much attack today. The do-away-with-God mentality of our age can't stand any of His ideas. Yet I'm writing to the man who is wise enough to recognize that God is always right. Archaeologically, scientifically (given a Creator God), historically and experientially (for millions of people), the Bible is accurate.

Nearly two thousand years ago, as the New Testament was being written, scientists were teaching that the earth was balanced on the back of a huge turtle. The great fear of the scientists of Rome was that the turtle would take a step and the world would go plunging into space. Yet if anyone had wanted to stop being afraid, they could have read the oldest book in the Bible, Job. "[God] hangs the earth on nothing" (Job 26:7). If it were going to fall, it would have fallen long before those Roman scientists had been born.

Voltaire, the French philosopher, once said, "A hundred years from now the Bible will be a forgotten book." Yet years later, when Voltaire was cold in the ground, the Geneva Bible Society was publishing Bibles in his former home.

I challenge any honest person "too intellectual" to believe the Bible to read the scholarly books of Josh McDowell, *Evidence That Demands a Verdict* (Volumes 1 and 2, Here's Life). If you remain honest and read McDowell, your life will never be the same.

Relationship Beyond Compare

In his outstanding book *Marriage, Divorce and Remarriage* (Baker Book House), Jay E. Adams describes marriage well: "God designed marriage to put an end to human loneliness, and to establish a companionship for both work and play that is beyond compare with any other human relationship available. Because of their individual differences, God decreed that marriage requires a man and a woman in every case."

Adams continues, "Marriage is a formal arrangement between two persons to become each other's loving companions for life. In marriage they contract to keep each other from ever being lonely so long as they both shall live."

So here's a big question for both the husband and the wife: Do you constantly work hard to keep each other from being lonely?

If the answer to the above question is no, you need to make changes—if you want your marriage to be blessed by God.

This is not to say that you will have no problems in your marriage. No trouble-free marriages exist. If you want to avoid all marriage problems, don't marry in January. And that goes for all of the other months of the year too!

To have no problems is an unrealistic goal. Realistically, there will be problems in any close relationship, and marriage is meant to be the closest of all relationships. When problems arise, you can't put Band-Aids on bullet holes and expect everything to be all right. Simplistic answers frustrate because they don't work. God's answers are never simplistic—though with His power many of them are simple to carry out. The great thing is, God's answers work.

Actually, solving marital problems can be fun. Consider a giant jigsaw puzzle or a crossword puzzle. Devoted fans will tell you that problems can be fun.

In marriage, solving each problem can teach a couple how to grow closer.

Again, here's God's promise to anyone who will honestly follow His directions: "If you abide in My Word, then you are truly disciples of Mine; and you shall know the truth, and [when you do it] the truth shall make you free" (John 8:31-32).

The Husband Is the "Head" of His Wife

"But I want you to understand that Christ is the head of every man, and the man is the head of a woman, and God is the head of Christ" (1 Cor. 11:3).

Headship is one of the least understood and most overused terms in the church world today. Many a hurting wife has been told by her church-going husband, "I'm head of the house, and you'll do what I say!" But headship is *not* synonymous with dictatorship. Headship is meant to give protection and blessing for the wife and family—and peace for the husband. It is not to "keep her in her place." Headship represents the spiritual authority a husband is to have over his wife and family, and the place Jesus Christ is to have over the husband. The husband who does not understand this and barks orders at his wife will end up living a dog's life!

For many centuries a twisting of 1 Corinthians 11:3 has led some to believe that men are the head of women. But the Bible teaches that "man is the head of a woman." It's hard enough to be the head of *one* woman. Don't try to be the head of them all!

If a man is married, the Bible declares that man is the spiritual head of his wife. If he has children, he is the spiritual head of each of them.

At a wedding the father is meant to give away his daughter (literally

118

giving away his spiritual headship over her) to her husband.

Hebrews 13:17 establishes pastors and elders of each congregation as spiritual heads for all people in their churches, instructing congregations to "Obey your leaders, and submit to them...as those who will give an account. Let them do this with joy and not with grief, for this would be unprofitable for you."

What is submission all about? Submission never means blind obedience to a dictator who sets his own rules and disobeys the Bible. Biblical submission is always to God Himself through Jesus Christ.

With that truth understood, let's define *submission* as an attitude of love that *wants* to cooperate.

This will be a far better world when the power of love replaces the love of power.

Who Sinned First?

To understand where we are, we need to look to our earliest ancestors, Adam and Eve. Who sinned first? Christian tradition has incorrectly placed the blame on Eve—for biting into the fruit. (Women often get wrongly blamed for things.) But a closer look reveals another answer.

According to the Bible, what causes death? Sin: "For the wages of sin is death" (Rom. 6:23). Who brought death into this world? Adam, not Eve. "For as in Adam all die..." (1 Cor. 15:22).

And for those who might argue that the name Adam in Hebrew means "man" (often referring to mankind or to the name given both Adam and Eve before the fall), 1 Corinthians 15:22 wasn't written in Hebrew, but in Greek. Here Adam is the name of the first man, as opposed to Eve, the name of the first woman.

According to 1 Timothy 2:14, Eve was completely deceived when she ate the fruit; she believed it was the right thing to do. Whereas Eve was deceived, Adam disobeyed. He walked into sin with his eyes wide open, and his sin caused death.

So what was the very first sin? Well, it couldn't have been the eating of the fruit. It was Eve who did eat first. But Adam sinned first—Eve sinned second. That means there had to be a sin that preceded the eating of the fruit. We read about Adam's sin in Genesis 3:17a: "Then to Adam [God] said, 'Because you have listened to the voice of your wife....'" *That* was the very first sin. Adam disobeyed and sinned against God because he listened to the voice of his wife rather than to the command of God.

I know some enthusiastic male reader is going to be shouting, "Hallelujah! You mean it's a sin to listen to the voice of my wife? I promise, I'll never do it again!" But that's not the point at all. What is the point? Second Corinthians 11:3 tells us Eve was beguiled or deceived. She really felt that that piece of fruit would make her more godly. Genesis 2:16-17 says that Adam had been given clear instructions by God *not* to eat from that tree: "And the Lord God commanded the man...." Eve was created after this command. Though both Adam and Eve were responsible to follow the command, Adam was responsible for being certain that Eve understood the command.

He was to repeat and study God's word with his wife. He was casual or negligent about this, as Eve had a garbled understanding of what the Lord had said. She told the serpent she wasn't to touch the fruit (see Gen. 3:2-3). God had never told Adam or Eve not to touch the fruit. His word was not to eat it.

Many Christians have never realized that Adam was standing right next to his wife during her conversation with the serpent. Genesis 3:6 says that after she bit into the fruit she handed it to Adam. How long do you suppose Eve's arm was? The New American Standard Bible is very specific about this. In Genesis 3:6 it reads, "She gave also to her husband *with her,* and he ate" (italics mine). Because Adam shirked his responsibility to follow God's command and take authority over his wife to protect her, the serpent destroyed the joy of the first marriage. Sin entered the world.

Submission to God's Word

The husband and the wife are to be fully submitted to both the written and the living Word, Jesus Christ. Adam and Eve's loss of paradise shows us how necessary communication with the Lord and each other is. Though "Christ is the head of every man" (1 Cor. 11:3) means that Christ is the husband's authority, this does not mean that a wife has to go through her husband to get to Jesus Christ. She has total access to the Lord at all times (see Matt. 7:7-8). But as the president of the United States has full authority as commander-in-chief of all armed forces, so Jesus Christ has full authority over every husband. He has orders for you so that you can win the war over Satan and his demon host. The tragedy is that in far too many church-goers' homes the husband and wife think the devil is each other!

The husband who believes biblical submission gives him the right to tell his wife to sin, and she "has to" submit to him, does not understand God's Word, as sin is never acceptable to God. Any wife who knowingly commits sin in order to "submit" to her husband puts herself in the same position as Sapphira in Acts 5:1-10. Sapphira was struck dead because she submitted to her husband and willingly joined in his sin.

Submission and Authority

Let's look at 1 Corinthians 11:3 once again: "But I want you to understand that Christ is the head of every man, and the man is the head of a woman, and God is the head of Christ."

Analyzed, that verse says:

God the Father is the authority of God the Son,
Who is the authority of the husband,
Who is the authority of his wife,
Who, in cooperation with him, is the joint authority of the children,
And the Holy Spirit cements all of these relationships
Together as the family submits to God's Word.

The first time I taught this, my son Tim was eight years old. Before bed that night he said, "Daddy, I didn't like that thing you taught tonight."

"What didn't you like?" I asked.

"I didn't like what you said about God the Father, and God the Son, and daddies and mommies. You didn't give me anything to be the authority over."

I believe the Holy Spirit gave me the words to say, "Your dog! You're the authority over your dog!"

With that encounter I saw that before Adam had been entrusted with a wife, God had given him authority over animals. And when God saw that He could trust Adam with caring for those animals, He was ready to let him be trusted with a wife.

Now the above paragraph in no way implies that I believe a wife is an animal! What I am saying is that anyone who wants or is granted authority must learn to take care of whomever or whatever he or she is the authority over. (I don't believe any child past the age of eight should be allowed to say that he or she "loves" a pet dog or cat or bird unless he or she is daily caring for that animal or bird.)

Let me define some words I've been using here: The biblical verb *submit* has, as one of its meanings, "To come under the protection of."

Someone has written, "God created Eve from Adam's rib. She wasn't made from his head so that she could be smarter than he. Nor was she made from his feet so that he could trample on her. She was taken out of his side so that they would be equal, under his arm to be protected by him, and near to his heart to be loved by him."

It's a tremendous responsibility to be the "authority," because you have to take care of whomever or whatever you are the authority over. What does authority mean? It is "the delegated right to exercise power."

Henry Brandt in his book *Balancing Your Marriage* describes well the husband-wife roles of authority:

> The relationship between wife and husband can be likened to the relationship between the President and Vice-President of a bank. Only one can be President. Both carry heavy responsibilities. The Vice-President knows the policies as well as the President. He [or in a husband-wife situation, she] helps make them, is in accord with them, and is limited in his decisions by them. Freedom comes through submission to bank policies. It is a friendly, inter-dependent relationship. Occasionally, new circumstances arise. The President calls his first Vice-President together to ponder the question. It's a serious moment when a meeting of the minds isn't possible. Such an occurrence is rare. But, when it comes, the President must make the final decision, not according to personal whim, but the best interest of the bank [again, in this case, the marriage]. Once the decision is made, everyone including the President, is bound by it. If later, the decision proves not to be in the best interest of the bank, it can be changed.[1]

James Walker in his outstanding book *Husbands Who Won't Lead and Wives Who Won't Follow* (Bethany House) writes about "the 'smothered' woman" "who is married to a man with the compulsive need to be in charge. She lives an uncomfortable, 'invisible' life and always feels she is unnecessary. Her husband may need her work, appreciate her ability to handle the children and be gratified by the sexual release she provides him, but her ideas—her needs, her wants and her soul—may seem uncared-for and ignored.'' A wife's utter dependence on the husband is not God's purpose in headship. Instead, His goal is to make the husband and wife a wonderfully efficient partnership.

Burn Your Whip and Chair!

If you have the idea that being the authority in your home means backing your wife into a corner and shouting "Back, wife! Back!," you have missed the whole idea. Headship does not mean a husband has the right to be the exclusive decision-maker or that he is always right when the spouses disagree.

Jesus Christ said it this way:

> Among the heathen, kings are tyrants and each minor official lords it over those beneath him. But among you it is quite different. Anyone wanting to be a leader among you must be your servant. And if you want to be right at the top, you must serve like a slave. Your attitude must be like my own, for I, the Messiah, did not come to be served, but to serve, and to give my life as a ransom for many (Matt. 20:25-28, LB).

Some husband reading this is bound to cry, "But I'm not Jesus Christ!" No, none of us is. But all Christians have been called to be like Jesus Christ (see Rom. 8:29). Though no human but Jesus Christ has ever been or ever will be "sinlessly perfect," our *attitude* is to be like His—*serving* those over whom we have authority, not *dictating* to them. This holds true for all who have biblical authority over anyone. Christ never has and never will make a selfish decision. Neither should we.

A couple came to see Bill Gaultiere for counseling. The husband, an aggressive, short-tempered, stubborn, noncommunicative workaholic, had married a woman whose personality was completely opposite to his. By nature she was sweet and submissive; when she arrived, she was extremely self-sacrificing, giving and emotionally a basket-case.

In tears, she said, "I work so hard to please him. I'm always giving up my needs to meet his. Then whenever we get into an argument, he says I have to submit to him! The more I give in, the more angry I get. I'm even mad at God. I just can't take it anymore.''

In defense of himself, the husband shouted at his wife, "Well, I'm the head of my house, and the Bible says you have to submit to me!" It took several sessions with this couple before the man recognized how wrong he had been about what submission means. He realized his insistent demand for his wife to submit to him had really been a way to avoid considering his wife's feelings, communicating and resolving their conflicts. In the setting of a Christian counselor's office, he found healing for his marriage by learning to communicate honestly with his wife. With her emotional needs now being met, her anger disappeared and she did not resist true biblical submission. Today they are both happy in their marriage. The same kind of miracles happen weekly during the Marriage Plus seminars.

The surest way for a husband to be certain his wife will not want to submit to him (or even God) is to tell her that the Bible says she "has to" submit.

Husband, if you want your wife to love you, serve her. Listen to her and consider her heart carefully before making decisions that affect your family. After you've prayerfully considered her viewpoint, you are to make the decision you believe Christ would have you make. God's whole idea in making you the family's head is for you to find and then do the will of God. It is never for you to make your family do *your* selfish will.

A wife who really loves Christ and knows her husband has listened to her and sought God for the right answers will surrender her will and submit. That is the picture of the Christian home.

The Problem of Missing Heads

I heard a comedian say, "I'm the head of my family, and my wife beats me with the belt." I started to laugh but stopped. Missing or wimpy husbands cause horrible family trauma. The comedian's comment wasn't funny but very sad.

Obviously, you have to be studying God's Word continually to know what His will is. And you have to be a man of prayer. The husband who says, "I'm too busy to do those things," can expect many heavy, unsolved problems until he finds the time.

A husband leads his wife by consciously investing his energies in ministering to her with God's love and his own. He willingly takes her to church, studies God's Word with her (by setting the daily schedule with her), offers to pray with her daily, plans regular date nights with her and sets those dates on his calendar "in concrete" so that nothing gets in their way. He remains a loving leader to the children and teenagers in his home too.

Let's look at five reasons why husbands don't take leadership roles in their homes.

1. *Husbands are too busy to lead.* Husband, your wife is a person, just as you are. She has human feelings that may even go deeper than your own. Today's husband often marries while still in school or at the beginning of a career. He steadily gives himself to his job, allowing his wife to play second fiddle. Communication breaks down, and the marriage breaks up.

Tell the Lord right now that this deterioration is not going to happen—or continue—in your marriage.

Many husbands are missing "the abundant life" (John 10:10) with their families by being like a magician's rabbit—constantly disappearing. By and large men today are overinvested in activities that in the long run will not pay. Elvis Presley couldn't drive one Rolls Royce after he was dead. Careers, money, a big name, knowledge, skills and climbing the ladder of success all get pretty shallow on a deathbed.

I stood at the bed of a dying man who told me, "Ray, if I just had it to do over again." His kids had broken his heart. He was divorced. He had spent all his time working and had nothing to show for it but money he couldn't take with him.

Men tend to derive much of their self-esteem from their accomplishments. This is normal. This healthy need to achieve becomes a problem only when it is not balanced with healthy, happy relationships. Remember? There is another basic male need: the respect of their wives. But when husbands fail to work at their marriages at least as hard as they work on their outside jobs, wives find respect difficult. Without Christ, she may not be able to find respect in her heart. With Christ, it will still be a challenge.

Husbands who spend too much time at work, routinely bringing work home with them or having trouble getting their minds off their work when they are at home, are likely to have frustrated wives. They often lose the leadership role by default—to the utter destruction of their families.

God's decree through Moses in Deuteronomy 24:5 underlines the absolute necessity of a man's need to learn how to spend both quantity and quality time with his wife: "When a man takes a new wife, he shall not go out with the army, nor be charged with any duty; he shall be free at home one year and shall give happiness to his wife whom he has taken." God, in His mercy, knows that a new wife is going to need cheering up!

Don't stay as busy as a bee, or you may wake up to find your honey missing!

2. *Husbands don't lead because they are afraid their wives won't follow.* Marriage counselor David Field in his book *Marriage Personalities* (Harvest House) refers to the active-passive marriage—the most common marriage pattern he sees in counseling. In the active-passive marriage a husband sits back passively and takes no active decision-making role in the family. At some point, because decisions have to be made by someone, the frustrated wife grabs the leadership role. She pushes and prods her husband—to give her more of his time, be more romantic, go to church or the couples' retreat, etc. This wife may be accused of being a women's libber, and her husband may call her a nag, but in reality she is just an unhappy wife with a husband who refuses to take the lead.

A husband who surrenders his God-given headship is a man who has quit obeying God. "For the husband is the head of the wife, as Christ also is the head of the church, He Himself being the Savior of the body" (Eph. 5:23). Notice again the purpose of headship is to be a blessing to your wife. You've been called to lead her and not abandon her as Adam did when Eve began to rebel.

First Corinthians 11:3, the verse that establishes the husband as head of his home, also calls Christ the man's Head. How can you get an unsubmitted wife to cooperate? Use your Head! A total surrender to Christ, patience in waiting on God's perfect timing, and walking in love and obedience to God's Word will be the most certain path to the miracle you long to see happen in your family.

3. *Husbands don't lead because they are hiding their own sin.* The husband who has a tendency to compare himself with others (including his "spiritual" wife) and feels like a failure will often have a devil-driven desire to shrink into a corner and hide. A low self-image, including the knowledge of his own sin, may make him feel that he could never help

his more spiritual wife grow in Christ. He may dig a deep hole for himself in alcohol or drugs and even feel a measure of acceptance by others who are doing the same thing. Or he may have an affair with someone who gives him a passing feeling of acceptance.

But there is always a major problem with sin, especially sexual sin that must be hidden. Along with the eternal consequences of unrepented immorality, the sinner has to live with himself. You can't take even a week's vacation away from your sin. The lies don't sleep. When you give it any thought, you know the cheap thrill isn't worth it. Of course, many an immoral person doesn't think—until their sins are discovered and come crashing down, destroying their children and their marriages.

4. *Husbands don't lead because they don't see the need.*

Some husbands just don't see the need to lead and support their wives. With the modern aggressive, independent image of women seeking personhood, many men feel no need to provide for them. As one husband told me, "My wife celebrates the Fourth of July every day of the year, because she is so independent!" He added, "If my wife just wants to be another man, I can walk out on her, and she can take care of herself."

Yet appearances can be deceiving. Behind the mask of independence a woman can be crying out for help. Inside every woman God has placed a desire to respond to a man's loving initiative and romantic pursuit. (Sometimes such feelings have been crowded out by the pain of some trauma, but these feelings can be restored by Jesus Christ.)

To fulfill His plan for marriage, God has created the man to enjoy winning his lady's heart. (Again, past emotional and/or demonic trauma may have buried these God-given feelings.) As you recognize your wife's need for you as her husband and begin spending concentrated time loving her, you will see how much she has needed you all along.

5. *Husbands don't lead because they are trying to escape.* Some husbands don't lovingly lead their wives because they feel smothered in their relationship. This was the case for Bob, who was about to divorce Sandy because he felt so trapped and frustrated. Sandy, who had already been divorced three times, lived in great fear of Bob walking out of the marriage.

Bob tried to pay attention to Sandy's feelings and prove his love, but the harder he tried to reassure her the more reassurance she seemed to need. Eventually Bob felt so overwhelmed with his failure to establish security in her that he wanted to give up. In response to Sandy's pleas for more and more of his time, he had all but abandoned the time he once spent building and flying remote-control planes—a hobby that had given him a great sense of accomplishment. His wife had a total monopoly on every minute of his free time.

The Lord saved this marriage just in the nick of time, as he led Bob to set limits. Bob had to be willing to say no to Sandy, to have some moments to himself. He had to let go of his guilt for not being able to please her all the time. Meanwhile, the Lord showed Sandy that she had to stop nagging Bob. She had to take responsibility for her own insecurities, letting the Lord minister to them. Ironically, once Sandy stopped pressuring Bob to give her more attention, he started to do it on his own. Now they fly remote-control planes together and are very much in love.

What About Being a Parent?

In 1 Samuel 2-4 Eli the priest felt that being in church was all the right training his children would need. He saw no need to "bring them up in the nurture and admonition of the Lord" (Eph. 6:4, KJV), as he was too busy with his clerical responsibilities. His kids turned out to be disasters, such disasters that God told Samuel, "And therefore I have sworn to the house of Eli that the iniquity of Eli's house shall not be atoned for by sacrifice or offering forever" (1 Sam. 3:14).

If I regret anything in this book, it is that I do not have room to teach on rearing children and teenagers. I spend more than two hours on this critically important subject during every Marriage Plus seminar. Arlyne and I plan to do a full book on this subject within the next two years. Meanwhile, see that your whole family is in a Christ-centered, Bible-believing and Bible-teaching church that will reinforce your efforts to fulfill Deuteronomy 6:6-7 and Ephesians 6:4. Your offspring are all you will ever have the opportunity to take to heaven with you. Invest your time, love and discipline, and "act upon" God's Word with them. No investment pays better dividends.

A Final Word on Headship

"Husbands, love your wives, just as Christ also loved the church and gave Himself up for her'' (Eph. 5:25).

Let me briefly summarize the issue of headship in a Christian marriage. The husband who follows Christ's example will humbly and generously put his wife's needs and interests before his own. He will give himself up for her just as Christ did for him. He will act upon God's Word, even when it isn't convenient.

A wife who really loves Jesus Christ and knows her husband has listened to her and sought God for His answers will surrender her will and submit. That is the picture of the Christian home.

ARGUING WITH YOUR WIFE IS AS USELESS AS TRYING TO BLOW OUT A LIGHTBULB!

Questions for Reflection and Discussion

1. Study Malachi 2:13-16 and Romans 1:28-32. In light of these two Scripture passages, consider the statement: ''In almost every divorce there is the covenant-breaker or 'untrustworthy' partner, who sinfully and often callously violates the commitment to his or her marriage covenant. Most often there is also the victim of the divorce, who has given every effort to keep his or her commitment to the covenant.'' How seriously does God view the agreement for both spouses to keep the wedding covenant? Are you working hard to keep yours?

2. Since God's first intention for marriage is to keep each spouse from ever feeling lonely (see Gen. 2:18), what are you doing to keep your spouse from feeling lonely? Separately from your spouse, write down three new things you could do together that would aid you both in a feeling of togetherness. Share your suggestions with each other.

3. Henry Brandt's illustration of how authority works in a bank is an excellent parallel to how the authority is meant to work in a Christian home. Think of a football or baseball team. Do all players have equal authority, or is there usually a captain? What is the role of the captain? Is the captain supposed to be submitted to the coach? What happens when that authority is misused or disregarded by the captain? (Again, see Matt. 7:24-27.)

Dear Ray,

You are a very funny man! I still listen to the Marriage Plus tape set at least once a month. Believe it or not, I still laugh at all your jokes. My wife still listens once a month too. I wish you could see us now. You wouldn't know us from the couple that sat in your Marriage Plus seminar two years ago and canceled our divorce before the week was over.

When I came to the seminar, I was hoping you'd get my wife straightened out. I really thought she was the one messing up our marriage. But I'll never forget my shock at your talk about the Christian husband. How far from that I was.

See, I never had a dad I could remember. My mom and dad were divorced when I was two. I lived with my mom and two sisters. I'd never figured out what a man really was—let alone a husband. It wasn't that I hadn't heard some teaching on what a man was. I had heard some. But somehow I thought a Christian husband had to be macho—kind of a Clint Eastwood or maybe Sylvester Stallone. When I heard you teach "The Christian Husband" I wondered—can this be true? Your careful teaching showed me it is. I used to think being tender or gentle meant being a wimp. Thanks, Ray. I don't feel that way anymore.

My wife used to hate my coming home from work every day. She told me so. Now she says it's the thing she most looks forward to. I don't mind writing you—we're in love! My kids even talk about hoping they can have a marriage as great as ours. They never talked that way until we came to your Marriage Plus seminar.

I'm not Clint Eastwood, but "You made my day." Thanks again,

A New Man in Christ

*"For the husband
is the head of the wife,
as Christ also is the head of the
church, He Himself
being the Savior
of the body."*

Ephesians 5:23

EIGHT

What's a Husband to Do?

TREAT YOUR WIFE LIKE A THOROUGHBRED AND SHE WON'T TURN OUT TO BE A NAG!

I recently read of a man who hadn't kissed his wife in five years. But he shot another man who did! That sounds just like me several years ago. I was totally neglecting my wife, miserable as could be in my marriage and hating my wife and myself. There is something in the despair of a marriage gone wrong that can't be equaled by any other pain. I didn't only hurt emotionally, I hurt physically. I could feel my bad marriage in the pit of my stomach. Even now, when there are a few minutes of tension between my wife and me, I can still feel that strain in my stomach.

We've already seen that God the Father is the authority of God the Son, who is the authority of the husband, who is the authority of his wife, who, in cooperation with him, is the joint authority of the children, and the Holy Spirit cements all of these relationships together as the family cooperates with God's Word. The husband being head of his wife is far more than an awesome power: it is an awesome responsibility. It's not that it's hard to do without coming under the lordship of Jesus Christ. It is *impossible* without coming under His lordship.

Jesus Christ told us,

> "Abide in Me, and I in you. As the branch cannot bear fruit of itself, unless it abides in the vine, so neither can you, unless you

abide in Me. I am the vine, you are the branches; he who abides in Me, and I in him, he bears much fruit; for apart from Me you can do nothing" (John 15:4-5).

The husband who feels he'll take the teaching of God's Word but not God has missed this point. We are not dealing with New Year's resolutions, but with the *living* Word of God (see Phil. 2:16; 1 John 1:1; Acts 5:20). Apart from Jesus Christ (see John 15:4-5) and the Holy Spirit in your life you can try to do the things a husband should do, and a few of them will work. But, like so many resolutions, your flesh will get in the way. You'll find it easy to quit and give up.

It is not that an unbelieving husband hasn't been given authority. It's that he lacks the necessary power to carry out the authority. *Authority* has to do with permission. *Power* is the ability to carry out the authority. Every husband has been granted by God the authority to be head of his house. But the power comes only by knowing God intimately through Jesus Christ (see John 1:12-14). Anyone might get the authority to drive a car. But to have power to drive a car a person must have the knowledge to drive and a fully equipped car.

The primary purpose of going to church is to receive the knowledge needed to live the Christian life and to be "equipped" with everything necessary for an "abundant life" (see Eph. 4:11-13; John 10:10). How can this happen if the pastor is out of order? This is the first qualification for a married church leader. "He must be one who manages his own household well, keeping his children under control with all dignity (but if a man does not know how to manage his own household, how will he take care of the church of God?)" (1 Tim. 3:4-5).

A pastor or church leader who says, "With all I have to do in the ministry, I can't see how I can also minister to my wife and kids," needs to repent quickly. His family is his first responsibility before the Lord. His congregation needs to realize and honor his responsibility. The pastor sets the example for the church.

Honoring Her

Ephesians 5:23 sits right in the middle of the three verses that very clearly tell wives they are to submit to their husbands. Look at the promise of

Ephesians 5:23: Jesus Christ is "the Savior of the body." Why does our Lord have Paul emphasize *that* as he's telling wives to submit to their husbands? Because that's what wives, as well as the church, are being promised. God is saying to wives, "Keep an attitude of always wanting to cooperate with your husband in any situation that isn't sinful (see Col. 3:18) and he'll be the savior of *your* body." The husband won't let his wife wear out spiritually, emotionally or physically.

In Jewish law a woman wasn't a person but an object more unnecessary in many ways than a cow. The late historian William Barclay wrote concerning the non-Christian world of the first century that a wife "had no legal rights whatsoever. She was absolutely in her husband's possession to do as he willed."[1] But biblical submission isn't like that at all. Peter wrote, "You husbands likewise, live with your wives in an understanding way, as with a weaker vessel, since she is a woman; and grant her honor as a fellow heir of the grace of life, so that your prayers may not be hindered" (1 Pet. 3:7).

The Greek word *honor* means "greatly value [her]; to recognize and reward [her] great worth." Husband, do you "greatly value" your wife? Do you "recognize and reward her great worth"? Does she know how much you love her? Do you keep telling her what a great woman she is? Are you watching out that she doesn't tire out? If not, these are the major reasons for the uncivil war going on in your marriage. And it's why your prayers are hitting the wall and falling on the floor unanswered. God's got a dead letter office for the prayers of those husbands who fail to follow His directions.

And what's this: "Live with your wives in an understanding way"? Peter wasn't asking the impossible. Husbands, you will not always understand your wives, but you can be understanding.

When a totally frustrated wife cries out to her husband, "You don't understand me, do you?" A husband often feels a need to defend himself: "Yes, I do." But inside is that awful truth, "No, I don't!" And the devil, "the accuser of the brethren" (Rev. 12:10), whispers in his ear, "Failure!" But nowhere does the Bible command a husband to understand his wife. God does command a husband to treat his wife "in an understanding way," whether he understands her or not.

I know some of you guys reading this are going to grab your Bibles like the lawyer who was about to die. The lawyer was searching the pages frantically. When asked what he was doing, the lawyer explained, "I'm looking for loopholes!" In his case, as well as your case, there aren't any loopholes. God tells it like it is.

In all Marriage Plus seminars I speak to husbands for a whole session and then to wives for a session, though the spouses are invited to listen in. When I speak to the wives, I ask them, "Are you obeying God? Are you faithfully choosing to cooperate with your husband in anything that isn't sinful?" If they aren't biblically submitting, they are like a sign hung on a pay phone: "out of order." But, men, unless you understand your part, the family will still be out of order. You have to do your part if she is to be able to do hers. "We love him, because he first loved us" (1 John 4:19, KJV). If you want your wife to love you, love her!

Your wife is no inanimate object. She is a human being loaded with feelings. Any man who thinks his wife should just roll over and play dead should have bought a dog instead of gotten married! Any guy who says, "I'd rather have a dog," doesn't understand the great value of his wife or how seriously God holds him responsible for the vows he said when he married her.

On the other hand, any wife who is underlining in this chapter so that she can use it on her husband is just going to make matters worse. The war will escalate. Husbands who haven't understood their biblical role usually do unto others before they get done unto!

Lights! Camera! Action!

Suppose you walked into your kitchen right now and found your refrigerator had turned into a toaster. Or suppose your toaster had turned into a refrigerator. You'd have disaster on your hands. After all, a refrigerator was made to be a refrigerator, and a toaster, a toaster. They function well only if they do what they were made to do. Even so, God has made husbands and wives so that they function well only if they do what God has created them to do. Each one has a definite role to play. Whatever you guys have been doing before, you can't sit in the audience and stare any longer. It's time to get on stage.

Since every Christian family member is to "act upon" God's Word, it's biblical to say that the husband and wife each has a role to play. The script is the Bible (see 1 John 1:1-3; Ps. 119:105; Is. 8:19-20; Eph. 1:13; et al.). The "Owner" of the "theater of life" is God (see Ps. 24:1-2; 1 Cor. 11:3; John 1:1-3; Rom. 11:36; and others). The "Star" of the theater is the One we must all try to imitate, Jesus Christ—He's the only One who has done the part perfectly (see Rom. 8:29; Eph. 4:11-13; Heb. 2:9-10; 5:8-9; and others). The "Director" is the Holy Spirit, who brings our lines or passages of Scripture to life so that we can follow the script (see John 14:26; 16:13-14; 1 Cor. 12:7-11; Is. 63:11-12). The most exciting thing about this whole production is that the Father, Son and Holy Spirit work in perfect harmony (see Luke 3:21-22; Gal. 4:6) to make the theater-of-life presentation more spectacular than you could ever imagine: "exceeding abundantly beyond all that [you] ask or think, according to the power that works within [you]" (Eph. 3:20). All you have to do is follow the script. On stage, husbands! Here's your part in the theater of life.

Loving Leader

When the Holy Spirit spoke through the apostle Paul and told your wife to submit to you, husband, He also told her you were to be like the Lord to her (see Eph. 5:22). So what is the Lord like?

"Since then we have a great high priest who has passed through the heavens, Jesus the Son of God, let us hold fast our confession. For we do not have a high priest who cannot sympathize with our weaknesses..." (Heb. 4:14-15a). Does your wife have a "priest" in her house like Jesus who "sympathizes with her weaknesses" instead of laughing at her or tearing her down? She should have. The verse continues: "...but one who has been tempted in all things as we are, yet without sin. Let us therefore draw near with confidence to the throne of grace, that we may receive mercy and may find grace to help in time of need" (Heb. 4:15b-16). Does your wife have a "great priest" who will give her "mercy" and "grace in time of need"? Again, she should have. You're to be like the Lord to your wife. Ready to listen to her and bless her. Wives don't want to be lorded over by their "lord."

One wife told me, "Home is where a husband goes when he's tired of being nice to people." What a sad definition.

The decisions Christ will lead you to make will be loving decisions, and most often your wife will agree with you. When you disagree, it's time to stop and find out why. Have you been less than loving toward her? Is the Holy Spirit ringing His alarm bell? Ephesians 4:29-32 explains,

> Let no unwholesome word proceed from your mouth, but only such a word as is good for edification according to the need of the moment, that it may give grace to those who hear. And do not grieve the Holy Spirit of God, by whom you were sealed for the day of redemption. Let all bitterness and wrath and anger and clamor and slander be put away from you, along with all malice. And be kind to one another, tender-hearted, forgiving each other, just as God in Christ also has forgiven you.

When a husband fails to act with love toward his wife but is unkind verbally or physically, he grieves the Holy Spirit. You need the Lord to work on your behalf, so don't grieve Him.

The Look of Love

> If I speak with the tongues of men and of angels, but do not have love, I have become a noisy gong or a clanging cymbal. And if I have the gift of prophecy, and know all mysteries and all knowledge; and if I have all faith, so as to remove mountains, but do not have love, I am nothing. And if I give all my possessions to feed the poor, and if I deliver my body to be burned, but do not have love, it profits me nothing (1 Cor. 13:1-3).

What is God's definition of love? The Greek word *agape* is the highest form of love—God's love for us. He expects it to be our kind of love for our wives, family and fellow man—always choosing to do God's highest good.

Husbands, stop for a minute and test your love quotient. Don't write your answers in the book, as your wife should take the test later.

A Love Test

"Examine me, O Lord, and try me; test my mind and my heart" (Ps. 26:2).

Ask yourself the following questions, but first heed two warnings: 1) If you are currently having tensions in your marriage don't take this test together or discuss your conclusions except in the presence of a wise Christian pastor or counselor. 2) As you reply, concentrate only on yourself, not on your spouse.

1. Are you patient with your wife (when she's shopping, etc.)?
2. Are you kind to her with your tongue? (Or do you put her down to her face or behind her back?)
3. Are you jealous or envious of your wife? (Is there any freedom or success of hers that you resent?)
4. Are you "boastful" (loud-mouthed)? (Do you shout angrily at your wife when you are frustrated?)
5. Are you proud (vain)? (Do you feel the world should revolve around you?)
6. Are you haughty, selfish or rude? (Blunt words often have the sharpest edges. Do you cut your wife off in midsentence to fire back a blunt word or unkind statement? Do you interrupt her? Do you ever tell her to shut up or swear at her?)
7. Do you demand your own way? (Is your idea of marriage a master-slave relationship? Or a mother-son relationship, where your wife ought to do everything for you?)
8. Are you irritable or touchy? (How do you speak to your wife when she interrupts your point of concentration? Do you lose your temper, or do you give her the attention she needs? How much of your body language shows her your disapproval or a lack of love?)
9. Do you carry grudges against your wife? (Do you fail to forgive her when she does something that disturbs you?)
10. Are you ever glad (secretly or otherwise) when your wife is treated unfairly? (Are you ever happy at the thought of your wife having an unpleasant experience that "serves her right"?)
11. Are you glad when truth wins out? (Do you accept the fact that she might be right about some things, and you might be wrong? How do you feel when that happens? When she "acts upon" God's Word, are you glad?)
12. Are you loyal to your wife? (Do you flirt with any other women or pay any attention to their flirting with you? Are you allowing any other human or thing to shove your wife into second place?)
13. Do you always believe in your wife and believe she'll do the right thing? (Do you trust your wife?)
14. Do you always stand your ground in defending her? (Do you quickly order any of your children, of whatever age, to apologize if they are rude to their mother? Do you ever let anyone talk negatively about your wife without defending her?)

Whatever your definition of love has been, the above questions are based on God's definition of *agape*:

> Love is very patient and kind, never jealous or envious, never boastful or proud, never haughty or selfish or rude. Love does not demand its own way. It is not irritable or touchy. It does not hold grudges and will hardly even notice when others do it wrong. It is never glad about injustice, but rejoices whenever truth wins out. If you love someone you will be loyal to him no matter what the cost. You will always believe in him, always expect the best of him, and always stand your ground in defending him (1 Cor. 13:4-7, LB).

Think carefully and prayerfully about each of the fourteen questions. You don't get a "B" on your paper if a few of your answers are off. If the answer to even one of these questions is different from what God says it should be, you have a problem in your marriage. Please don't shrug that problem off or try to make excuses for it. Most people who are failures are experts at making excuses. Please don't feel condemned—a heavy feeling in your heart that there is nothing that can ever be done about the problem, and you are cursed with it for life. Do feel convicted—the knowledge you'd better do something to correct the situation and change your ways.

Now your wife also should take the quiz. But remember, if there is any tension in your marriage, a test like this, when discussed without a wise, Christ-centered counselor present, can cause greater problems than you already have. Every verbal attack you make on your spouse will mean lost ground in your marriage.

The apostle Paul said marriage is the closest parallel to the walk we humans have with Jesus Christ (see Eph. 5:22-31). In the longest passage of Scripture defining the husband's role, Paul outlines the major considerations necessary in being a husband who will be easily loved by his wife.

As Christ Loved the Church

> "Husbands, love your wives, just as Christ also loved the church and gave Himself up for her" (Eph. 5:25).

Self-centeredness—downright selfishness—is the number-one killer of marriages today. Has your wife become an appendix to you, someone to have sex with when it's convenient? Someone to keep the house tidy? Someone to keep your kids in line? Then you have abandoned God's assignment.

I know men who will spend hour upon hour making fish flies, polishing their rifles or practicing their putts. But they'll totally neglect their most important treasures, their wives. Wives will never be as interested in your fame, in your wealth or in your possessions as they will be in your attention.

Romance is as essential to a great marriage as air is to lungs. Romance includes holding your wife, helping her set the table, walking the baby so your wife can take a nap and a thousand other ways of saying "I love you." Say the words *I love you* every day. But romance is different strokes for different folks. I howled with hilarity at what a guy in England once did. He put a Valentine message in the *London Times*: "To Debbie Pookie People Pips from Petey Popsy Pooples—I love you—be mine." I don't know who Debbie Pookie People Pips is, but I sure hope she was impressed.

In the Marriage Plus seminar I spend an hour teaching what romance means and how to be a romantic husband. One of the best available books on marriage is *Help! I'm a Pastor's Wife* (Creation House), compiled and edited by Michele Buckingham. It includes a chapter by my darlin' Arlyne on how she and I keep the romance alive in our marriage. Arlyne often speaks to husbands while I speak to the wives. You'll see why the guys profit from that session when you read some of her wisdom, quoted from her chapter in Michele's book. First Arlyne talks about "practicing love":

> Today, I can honestly say that Ray and I love each other more than ever. More than on our wedding day. We've practiced loving. How do you practice loving? For Ray and me, practice takes many forms. Sometimes we're silly, laughing together and having great fun. Other times we're passionate and intense. Sometimes we're tender and quiet, giving each other "space." Other times we're partners, tackling a project together for the pure joy of working side by side.
>
> It was wonderful to realize, in those early days of putting our marriage back together, that romance is not necessarily the same for each person or couple. When Ray and I paint the house together, I feel romantic. Not many other women do! What I've learned

is this: I'm not bound to initiate and respond romantically in the same way as my best friend, my next door neighbor or the woman on the soap opera. I'm not someone else!

Ray isn't someone else either. He doesn't have to fill the living room with flowers—just because some TV Romeo did—to show me he cares. He has his own ways, and I'm learning to appreciate them....

We've had to develop our own unique style of romantic love. Developing that style has required, first of all, communication. We've had to make the extra effort to tell each other what our needs and desires are....For example, until we shared our romantic likes and dislikes, Ray had no idea that I felt special when he repaired a light fixture or worked on some other malfunctioning household item. Yet these small activities made me feel protected and cared for. At the same time, it never occurred to me that Ray really liked it when we watched television together. I figured since we weren't talking during the show, it didn't matter if I was there or not. But to Ray, it mattered.

A lot of people ask how Arlyne and I keep the spark alive in our romance since I travel so much for ministry and we've often had to be apart. Now Arlyne often travels with me, too, because our kids are grown. But, speaking for the years when she was home nearly all the time, Arlyne answered:

As Ray's ministry has expanded, we've had to concentrate on keeping the romance alive. His travels now take him away from home for periods of three or four weeks or more. Absence does not necessarily make the heart grow fonder! When he's ministering out of town or overseas and I'm at home with the children, it's easy to think separation is "normal." We have to fight against this.

When Ray is traveling he calls or writes every day. It's important that he be constantly informed of the daily home routine, my successes and failures and the children's needs and activities. It's just as important that the children and I know what he is doing, whom he is with and the things the Lord is accomplishing in his ministry. He needs to be and feel a part of us, and we need to be and feel a part of him. Usually he calls at a scheduled time, but sometimes he calls when I least expect it—and usually just when I really need to talk to him.

Both Arlyne and I know that romance can require sacrifice. (Remember Sir Walter Raleigh? He spread his cape in the mud so a woman could step on it instead of in a puddle. How's that for romance?) Arlyne continues,

> Accommodation often takes a large dose of self-sacrifice. For example, I love to shop, and Ray will sometimes go with me. We both enjoy browsing through a mall or a few specialty shops. It's relaxing exercise as well as a change of scenery. When I look at women's clothing, however, I know it's not easy for him! But patiently and politely, he gives me his opinion on the outfits I try on. When we find something we both like, he enjoys buying it for me. How I appreciate him at those times!

At one of our recent seminars Arlyne added, "You don't always have to be talking to be loving. Spaces in conversation are natural and normal, and many people require time to be alone without any need to communicate, moments when you're not responsible to anybody except God."

When I'm home Arlyne or I—alone—may go out and walk through a shopping mall. (I like to do that. Most men don't!) Sometimes we find a present to take to the other. We both enjoy this. But, far more than that, Arlyne and I enjoy going out together—walking our dogs Taffy and Casey.

The point is, wanting to be alone without each other all the time would indicate a problem. But "spaces" in our communication or in our bodily togetherness aren't wrong. For you, an occasional fishing or hunting trip with men whose morals are respected by both husband and wife can be good and healthy. For her, a week of visiting out-of-town parents when you honestly can't get off work is fine.

The rule should be: If either partner does feel a need to be away, it should happen only with the full, comfortable, nondemanding OK of the spouse who is going to be left. In almost every day of your marriage there should be enough time for both aloneness and communication.

Dating Your Wife Is Essential

One of the reasons why many singles are staying single these days is because they like to date. They see that dating stops when people get married. After all, they've never seen their parents date each other. How tragic and how foolish! Guys, dating should never stop.

At every Marriage Plus seminar I mention our surprise nights. Arlyne writes about them:

> At least once a month we have a "Surprise Date Night." Ray will tell me the day, the time and how to dress—nothing more. We may go to a play, a movie, the beach—or out to dinner, for a long drive or any combination of these. Sometimes I am the one who does the planning and surprising. We both eagerly anticipate this special time of talking, relaxing, focusing on each other and just having fun! While we plan, we also try to be open for an unexpected lunch out, a quick excursion, or a quiet time together.

Arlyne and I love going to plays together. Glendale Centre Theatre in Southern California has some of the best presentations anywhere and extremely low prices for such entertainment. They change plays about every six weeks, and we try never to miss one. Sometimes our kids join us, or some of our close friends. Dinner before the show is a must, to allow time for happy communication.

Being romantic is contagious. It's been fun to see our kids pick up on romantic date ideas of ours. Tim wooed Kelly with many a creative date that led to their marriage. Both David and Bethany are romantics. They're interested in the sheer fun of dating with very special Christian friends. This makes for great experiences and memories and builds solid relationships.

Cultivating Friendships

"A mirror reflects a man's face, but what he is really like is shown by the kind of friends he chooses" (Prov. 27:19, LB).

When I am home from travel, you can be sure Arlyne and I will spend evenings with some of our closest friends. I cultivate these friendships. Typically, we'll go out for dinner, either in a restaurant or at someone's home. One of our best friends is a gourmet cook. Another, a deputy sheriff, makes the best Mexican salsa I've ever tasted. Arlyne, herself, gets rave reviews for anything she cooks, and I like to barbecue. So we can't miss if we eat at one of their homes—or ours.

We catch up on what each of us has been doing while we've been apart. There'll be plenty of laughter, some serious concern over any problems shared and a magnificent feeling that any of us could share our deepest, darkest secrets and these friends would know how to minister to us—or we to them. After dinner we usually drive to a frozen yogurt shop nearby for dessert. Then back to the house for more visiting, playing games and prayer. I'm not sure how some couples make it without close, Christ-centered friends. If you don't have at least two or three couples to share and pray with, begin asking God for them, and don't stop until you're sure you've found them.

But I Travel for a Living

If you are in the military or some other occupation like my own that requires you to travel and be away from your spouse: (1) Be sure you are where the Lord wants you to be. (2) Be sure you both agree that the Lord wants you there. I would never have become a traveling Bible teacher except that Arlyne and I *knew* (and know now) that the Lord has called me to do this. (3) Keep daily communication with each other as much as is humanly possible.

Even when I'm overseas I write Arlyne at least a letter a day. I send her lots of picture postcards, and I phone at least once a week. It's important that you "reach out and touch someone"—especially if that someone is your wife. Even if you don't like to write (most men don't), it's vital that you regularly communicate with her about what's going on in your life.

Even my widowed mother gets a postcard from me regularly. My point is, if you must be away, even for long seasons, you can still keep your family first.

A couple of guidelines about what to say—and not to say—when you write home. Talk love talk. That doesn't necessarily mean you have to be gooey. It means don't say anything you could regret. The pen is mightier than the sword—so don't stab each other! If you're blue for some reason, be cheerful in your letter anyway. "A joyful heart is good medicine" (Prov. 17:22). The point of writing a letter to your spouse should be to make her feel better for having received it. Bills don't excite the receiver; neither do gloomy, complaining, unhappy letters. Keep the tone of a letter (or love note that you leave her when you go off to work) loving, sincere and Christ-centered. Even if for some reason you have to convey unpleasant news, keep God's Word in perspective. All things do eventually "work together for good to those who love God, to those who are called according to His purpose" (Rom. 8:28). Today is probably not the last day of your life, just one of the days in your life. So look to the bright tomorrow if it's raining on your parade today—and give your reader a good-weather forecast.

P.S. The first time you write a love note to your wife and leave it for her in your house, be sure you address her by her given name. Otherwise she's likely to think she found something!

If you know the Lord wants you to be on the road, then you are under His call—and His promise (see Matt. 19:29). My call to travel has required sacrifices and tears from all of us. I missed Tim's ordination into the ministry. I missed seeing David and his friends win first place for a scene they did from "MacBeth" in competition with thirty-two high schools. I missed hearing Bethany sing a solo with the Church on the Way youth choir. We've grieved because I wasn't there.

But God has ways of making up for our sacrifices. We had many long summer ministry trips together as a family. In 1977 He sent our whole family to live an entire year in New Zealand. After high school David spent a full year traveling with me as my ministry assistant. Summers during college Bethany has worked closely with me as my personal secretary. Tim got me started doing Singles Plus seminars. He still advises me on art layouts for brochures and the like. Most wonderful of all, today my children are following Jesus Christ. Now that the kids are grown, Arlyne can travel with me. God has been faithful.

The Sanctifying Spouse

Let's now look at Ephesians 5:25-27:

> Husbands, love your wives, just as Christ also loved the church and gave Himself up for her; that He might sanctify her, having cleansed her by the washing of water with the word, that He might present to Himself the church in all her glory, having no spot or

wrinkle or any such thing; but that she should be holy and blameless.

The amazing truth is that whichever spouse is a Christian following God's directions "sanctifies" the spouse who is not believing God (see 1 Cor. 7:14). But what a difference it makes when two believers are following God. The power of two agreed in prayer is awesome (see Matt. 18:19). When two are agreed on the road map of life, the Bible, you've got an unbeatable couple.

The word *sanctify* means "to set apart for special attention." Does your wife have your "special and unique attention"? If not, it's time to repent and sanctify your wife.

Television, your computer, sports, work, organizations, hobbies— nothing is to be more important to you than the Lord, your wife and your offspring.

If you'll take this following pledge, husbands (and wives), you'll get high marks in sanctifying your spouse: "I will never make my spouse feel she [or he] is in competition with anything or anyone else in my life."

Say it. But, more important, mean it.

Love Her; Love Yourself

The Ephesians 5 passage continues with a further word to husbands:

So husbands ought also to love their own wives as their own bodies. He who loves his own wife loves himself; for no one ever hated his own flesh, but nourishes and cherishes it, just as Christ also does the church, because we are members of His body (vv. 28-30).

It is the great desire of Jesus Christ, husbands, that you feel good about yourselves, though not conceited. (Even Zsa Zsa Gabor said, "Macho is not mucho!") He wants you to recognize the joy of headship as you see your kids headed in the right direction, following the Lord. He wants your wife to want to lay her head on your strong shoulder. It feels good to feel good. Nourishing your family with the Word of God and letting your wife know you cherish her will go a long way in establishing the kind of home you'll be proud to head.

Leave to Cleave

Ephesians 5:31: "For this cause a man shall leave his father and mother, and shall cleave to his wife; and the two shall become one flesh" (Eph. 5:31).

"Planned parenthood" shouldn't mean a debate over which parent's home you plan to live in! When you marry, you need to stand on your own four feet following Jesus Christ. No comparing your wife's pie with your mom's pie, guys, unless your wife's pie is better. If it is better, tell your wife, but not your mom. (No more comparing your husband's weaknesses with your father's strengths either, wives!)

It is true that Ephesians 5:31 speaks of the husband leaving his parents, but not the wife leaving hers. However, that's only because the Jewish people knew the bride always left her parents once she was married (see Gen. 24:3-8; 34:16; et al.). One of the expressions most used among the Jewish people was to "take a wife." One wife told me, "I know I sure got taken when I got married!"

A Final Word to Husbands

"This mystery is great; but I am speaking with reference to Christ and the church. Nevertheless let each individual among you also love his own wife even as himself; and let the wife see to it that she respect her husband" (Eph. 5:32-33).

Showing honest respect for her husband is the single most important ingredient in the wife's relationship to her husband. He'll earn that respect as he follows God's directions for the Christian husband.

**A HUSBAND WHO SITS UNDER A TREE
WHILE HIS WIFE MOWS THE LAWN
COULD BE CALLED A "SHADY CHARACTER"!**

Questions for Reflection and Discussion

1. What is the difference between acting upon God's Word, as described

in the section "Lights! Camera! Action!," and being a phony? What ingredients will make the difference? Before formulating your written answer, read Colossians 3:12; John 1:12-13; Acts 1:8; and Matthew 7:24-27.

2. What does it mean for the husband to be "like the Lord" to his wife? In formulating your written answer, read Ephesians 5:23, 25; Hebrews 4:14-16; and Romans 8:29.

3. What does Arlyne mean when she says that we "practice love"? What does she mean by "developing our own unique style of romantic love"? After defining both of those statements, list four ways you are now practicing love. List four ways you will develop your unique style of romantic love with your spouse. Talk these ways over together and get his or her reaction.

4. Husband, write a love letter to your wife and mail it to her. Then for the next three weeks, on different days of the week, leave a love note at home so that she will find it after you are gone. (Be sure to use her first name!) Write down her responses to each.

5. Plan four surprise nights (as described in this chapter) for your wife and carry them out during the next four months. Write down her responses to each.

Dear Ray,

I was in your seminar in Oregon three years ago. I loved it. I just want you to know what has happened as a result. Our son, Frank Jr., just graduated from high school with a full-tuition scholarship to the nearby university. That is a miracle. Three years ago Frankie was an unhappy high school freshman already into drugs. My husband and I were brokenhearted over him, but we didn't know what to do. Actually my husband and I were fighting so much with each other that we didn't have a lot of positive effect on Frankie in spite of the fact that we loved him and went to church.

I was into women's lib—hook, line and sinker. My husband was just a big joke to me. I was tired of him, felt he was a weakling, hated his chauvinism and probably would have been a pretty good candidate for an affair—except that I hated men. Let's face it, I was a mess.

When I heard you were going to talk on submission, I figured I just wouldn't go. But I got roped into it by one of my friends. She had planned four of us going out to lunch afterward. I didn't feel I could miss that, so I went but figured I wouldn't listen. Well, my friend got saved that day. And I got to hear what God says about submission. My friend got saved and my marriage got saved.

I was wrong about a lot of things. I've got a great husband. Frankie straightened out shortly after I straightened out. God is sure good, isn't He? Thanks.

Changed and Happy

*"Wives, be subject
to your own husbands,
as to the Lord. For the husband
is the head of the wife, as Christ
also is the head of the church,
He Himself being the
Savior of the body.
But as the church
is subject to Christ,
so also the wives ought
to be to their husbands in
everything."*

Ephesians 5:22-24

NINE

The Wife
Who Uses Her Head

OH, WHAT A DAY WE LIVE IN! THE OLD-FASHIONED GIRL
WHO USED TO DARN HER HUSBAND'S SOCKS NOW HAS A
DAUGHTER WHO SOCKS HER DARN HUSBAND!

Genesis 1:27 says, "And God created man in His own image, in the image of God He created him; male and female He created them." Verse 28 continues, "And God blessed *them*; and God said to *them*, 'Be fruitful and multiply, and fill the earth, and subdue it; and rule over...every living thing that moves on the earth' " (italics mine).

Biblical submission and partnership in marriage go hand in hand. In any marriage, only when men and women work together is there ultimate success.

It's not surprising that Adam was created first. A great designer always makes a rough copy before he makes a masterpiece! You see, men are *not* better than women. Men are certainly *not* more important in God's sight. The promises of God's Word will work as quickly for any woman as they will for any man.

Galatians 3:28, "...there is neither male nor female; for you are all one in Christ Jesus," is often used as a battle cry for unisex. But God has made woman indispensable as an individual sex. In fact, to throw away her individuality would be to threaten all of mankind.

Yet today many a wife is asking, "What is my purpose in life?" Rodney Dangerfield isn't the only one who "ain't got no respect!" I talk with frustrated wives every week. Their complaint often goes something like this: A guy works hard and keeps getting raises. Everyone from his boss to his secretary tells him how great he's doing. But a wife who stays home and faithfully dusts, vacuums, irons, washes clothes, makes beds, wipes the baby's nose (and other parts), referees the children, shops for bargains to save money for her family, attends PTA meetings, cooks, makes cupcakes for the Cub Scouts and does a thousand other thankless jobs gets no raises. Instead all she hears from her husband is that she spends too much money. And he wonders what she does with all that "free time" she has.

There are several ways that such a woman who lacks purpose in life might try to deal with her problems.

1. She could get a job in the work force and let her kids be raised by someone else while she and her husband grow more frustrated with each other because she stays so tired.

2. She could have an affair. Some guy is obviously available who would hold her in his arms and whisper sweet nothings in her ear. She would have to live with herself, lying to her husband and kids, to her pastor, even to God. She would know she was violating everything God stands for, and she'd feel cheap and condemned under the constant fear of being found out.

3. She could get a divorce, but since only 11 percent of husbands in America pay alimony, a divorce would almost certainly force her to abandon the children to someone else while she exhausted herself trying to make ends meet. And God "hates divorce" (Mal. 2:16), knowing the pain it causes all parties.

4. She could continue in the misery she knows now and keep complaining to her husband about how unfair life seems.

5. She could realize that this is the first day of the rest of her life and make Jesus Christ Lord of her circumstances, trusting Him and acting upon God's Word until abundant life becomes a reality for her, her husband and their family.

As you might imagine, Arlyne and I recommend the last option, which certainly isn't the most popular these days. Anyone reading this may be hearing from someone else, "Honey, we women only get one ride on this merry-go-round of life, and we aren't getting any younger. Reach for the gold ring. Grab all the gusto you can!" But before you swallow that line, ask yourself why two-thirds of all women with master's degrees in business have left the managerial work force. *Fortune* magazine says it's because they've refused to juggle a professional career life with a family.[1]

Many voices are screaming out for women's attention today, only one of those voices isn't screaming. It is God's voice, and He still speaks in a still, small voice only discernible when you study and hear God's Word (see Rom. 10:17). The rest of the voices are stumbling blocks because they center on selfishness rather than on following God.

When Peter rebuked Christ because our Lord said He was going to give up His life for you and me, Jesus rebuked him in return, "Get behind Me, Satan! You are a stumbling block to Me; for you are not setting your mind on God's interests, but man's" (Matt. 16:23).

Just as Jesus Christ knew His purpose in life and what He would accomplish by fulfilling His purpose (see Phil. 2:5-11), so each wife has great purpose. Yes, it includes a cross. The cross may be a cross husband! His anger, swearing, depression, false accusations, wrong choices, sin and lack of understanding may be enough to make her feel as if life isn't worth living. It is sometimes hard to recognize such problems as a smoke screen from hell to make her think she will never find the abundant life described in John 10:10.

The cross was an ugly challenge to Jesus Christ. Luke tells us that "His sweat became like drops of blood" (Luke 22:44) the night of His betrayal. But He went there because He knew His Father's will (see John 8:28-29).

So the real question is, wife, what path will you choose? Here's what Jesus said about your decision: "If anyone wishes to come after Me, let him deny himself, and take up his cross, and follow Me. For whoever wishes to save his [or her] life shall lose it; but whoever loses his [or her] life for My sake shall find it" (Matt. 16:24-25).

There are basically two ways for a woman to be assured success in life. One way is to put her shoulder to the wheel. The other way is to put her head on the shoulder of the man at the wheel. God calls on every wife to use her head!

The apostle Paul made a statement that some may have difficulty with: "For man does not originate from woman, but woman from man; for indeed man was not created for the woman's sake, but woman for the man's sake" (1 Cor. 11:8-9).

This doesn't mean a wife was designed to be her husband's slave. Woman was created for man because God saw the need in man—not the need for slave labor to help him run the garden but the need for companionship. God created woman for man's sake because man was lonely.

We've already looked at Paul's word to husbands in Ephesians 5:25: "Husbands, love your wives, just as Christ also loved the church and gave Himself up for her." Men are instructed to give themselves up for their wives and to meet their need for love. Women are to respect their husbands and meet their need for companionship.

In God's design a wife has two special purposes. They are outlined in Genesis 2:18 (LB), "And the Lord God said, 'It isn't good for man to be alone; I will make a companion for him, a helper suited to his needs.' " So a wife is to be 1) her husband's best friend and fun companion and 2) the "helper" designed to meet her husband's needs.

A wife who misses on those two points, that is, one who isn't a fun companion to her husband and "a helper suited to his needs," will have an ache inside no matter how well everything else is going.

Best Friend and Fun Companion

How can you be your husband's best friend? Few people married for love during Bible days. Marriages were prearranged by parents of the prospective bride and groom. Remember *Fiddler on the Roof?* Love had to be "learned." As Titus 2:4 indicates, it often had to be learned after the marriage had already taken place. The couple learned to love each other.

"Older women likewise are to be...teaching what is good, that they may encourage the young women to love their husbands, to love their children" (Titus 2:3-4).

A weeping wife came to see me before one of my seminar meetings and said, "Ray, I must be the worst wife and mother in the world. I don't love my husband. And worse—I don't believe I love my children either. I'm a horrible person, aren't I?"

I said, "No. You're a very normal person."

She gasped, "How can you say that after I just told you I don't love the members of my own family?"

I had her turn to Titus 2:3-4. When she read it the light began to dawn. Then we discussed the Greek word translated as *love* in Titus 2:4. She began to see that she had been looking for the feeling of love. God did not demand that she have a feeling. Rather, He was asking her to *learn* how to love her husband and children, then let the feelings take care of themselves.

Raymond Chandler, author of *The Maltese Falcon*, wrote, "However perfect the honeymoon, the time will come, however brief it is, when you will wish she would fall downstairs and break a leg! That goes for him, too! But the mood will pass if you give it time." Mr. Chandler was right on.

The Greek word for love in Titus 2:4 is not *agape*, as in the Ephesians 5:25 command for husbands to love their wives. It is the Greek word *philandros,* which means "to be a friend."

To learn to love you've got to act it (Matt. 7:24-25) until you feel it. I'm asked at nearly every seminar, "How did you begin to feel love for Arlyne if you didn't have any love for her when you married her?"

First, Arlyne is a very lovable person. She made it as easy for me as she knew how. But even if she hadn't been lovable, and I had had to win her love, Colossians 3:14 gives the whole key: "put on love."

"And beyond all these things put on love, which is the perfect bond of unity" (Col. 3:14). Every married person must "put it on," performing "love" in every way as if it were true even if it is only acting on the Word until it is true. It may sound like a silly phrase, but fake it until you make it. You will make it if you keep on keeping on. You will begin to feel and then continue to grow in a deep love for your spouse. Pray as you act on God's Word, and ask Him to give you love for your husband (or wife).

Godly love is learned by being obedient to God's Word. When a wife does what she is meant to do, in praying, giving herself, submitting, communicating and so forth, she will learn to love her husband. God will see to that. In time she will feel a deep love for her husband (or children) that this world, without Christ, can't even comprehend. God is faithful.

Although a man should have good male friends, none can replace his wife. God, in order to meet the loneliness in a man's life, knew what man needed. It wasn't an excellent group of male friends. It was a wife. "He who finds a wife finds a good thing" (Prov. 18:22).

In *Covenant Relationships* Keith Intrater writes,

The words "helper comparable to him" [see Gen. 2:18] in the

Hebrew are "ezer k'negdo." This expression literally means a helper that is opposite to him. In many ways, men and women are opposites. God sees a husband and wife as two members of a composite team. God will often draw together a man and a woman whose personal qualities are directly in contrast to one another. In this way the marriage partner will fill in the complementary personality gaps of the other. The two of them together will reflect the whole character of God.[2]

God deserves to be expressed through femininity, not just through masculinity. Wives supply the tenderness, the softness, the feminine mystique. They supply all those things that make men joke about not being able to understand women, and all those things that would be destroyed in one generation if women's lib and the unisex movement should ever take over.

Just as Eve was taken from Adam and left him incomplete until she became "one" with him again (see Gen. 2:23-25), so a husband is incomplete without his wife.

It's true. Your husband can't figure you out. But he knows he needs what you contribute. He's empty when he's away from you.

A man needs his wife, not just for companionship, not just for sex, but for the completion of his entire personality. Let that knowledge give you confidence in yourself as a wife. Your husband needs you.

A wife isn't called to "remake" her husband, but her husband, through her, will be made complete.

The Titus Five

We looked at Titus 2:3, which gives instruction for what experienced wives should teach younger women. In the following verses Titus lists five more qualities:

"Older women likewise are to...[teach] what is good, that they may encourage the young women to love their husbands, to love their children, to be [1] sensible, [2] pure, [3] workers at home, [4] kind, [5] being subject to their own husbands, that the word of God may not be dishonored" (Titus 2:3-5).

1. *Sensible people are discreet—careful about what they say or do.* They

neither gossip nor encourage gossip. They preserve confidences when necessary and can be trusted with privileged information, sharing it with no one but God. No one can sling mud with clean hands!

Some men are known gossips. But because of two factors having to do with the right side of the brain—verbal communication and a desire for relationships—ungodly women are more prone to gossip than men. It's been said, "Conversation is when three women are talking. Gossip is when one of them leaves." God forbids gossip (see Titus 2:3). Christian wives are to be sensible and discreet. (So are we all!)

2. *A pure wife walks in physical holiness, preserving her sex life only for her husband* (see Heb. 13:4). When David violated God's law and committed adultery with Bathsheba, he pleaded with God to be restored to "a clean [or pure] heart" and to be renewed to a committed spirit (Ps. 51:10). There is an honest innocence about anyone who has a pure mind and heart. A pure person will often be honestly dumbfounded to discover something sinful said or done by someone else because "to the pure, all things are pure" (Titus 1:15). Pure people don't go around looking for sin, and they are shocked when they find it. They aren't looking for faults in other people.

3. *Christian wives are meant to be "workers at home."* God is able to gift all wives in homemaking skills. If you are a wife wishing you could be a homemaker, know that your wish is a calling from God. It is as natural for you to desire to be a homemaker as for a fish to desire to be in water. The Greek word used for *workers* in "workers at home" is a word from God to let you know He thinks homemaking takes a lot of time to do well. The factory that produces the most important products is the home.

4. *Titus says a Christian wife is to be kind.* Kind actions begin with kind thoughts. Ephesians 4:32 clearly defines what kindness means in God's vocabulary: "And be kind to one another, tender-hearted, forgiving each other, just as God in Christ also has forgiven you." Being a wife can seem like a thankless job. Yet unkind people need kindness the most. A lot of women are wisely into exercise today, and Titus 2:5 says Christian wives should exercise kindness. (Husbands, the only exercise some men get is jumping to conclusions and running down their wives! Instead, you be kind too.)

5. *The final word to Christian wives in Titus 2:5 is that they be "subject*

to their own husbands, that the word of God may not be dishonored.''
There may be a lot of things said pro and con regarding submission. But
this clearly gives God's reason for His command to wives. First Samuel
15:23 (LB) says, ''For rebellion is as bad as the sin of witchcraft, and
stubbornness is as bad as worshiping idols.'' If I advised either Satan worship or the worship of anything or anyone other than God, you'd be wise
to burn this book. Well, rebellion against God's plan for you (submission) is as bad as witchcraft, and being stubborn toward God's plan (by
being stubborn toward cooperating with your husband in anything but sin)
is as bad as dedicating your worship to any idol.

The world is talking about churchgoers today, and most of the world
is saying they can't see much difference between lost people and Christians. That is because so many churchgoers' homes are out of order. Wife,
''Let your light so shine before men, that they may...glorify your Father
which is in heaven'' (Matt. 5:16, KJV).

The High Cost of Not Submitting

I've heard women say, ''Oh, I've tried that submission stuff! It doesn't
work.'' But if I find out more about them, I usually discover they don't
like being humble before the Lord (see 1 Pet. 5:6-7); they don't do much
Bible study looking for answers (see John 15:7); they don't spend much
time in prayer (Luke 18:1); and they only ''tried'' submitting for a little
while (Gal. 6:9). But let me list three high costs to families where wives
are unsubmitted: (1) Unhappy marriages. I've talked to plenty of husbands.
In confidence they have unloaded their miseries. (2) Sassy, insolent teenagers. By the time the children have become teenagers, they feel they have
the right to shoot off their mouths at any time. Their actions are a learned
response. (3) Divorce is rampant among families where the wife is
unsubmitted.

What Biblical Submission Isn't

A woman who heard that I was going to speak on the subject of biblical
submission told me, ''I don't want to hear it. Whenever I hear someone
say that I need to submit to my husband I think of my parents' relationship. He treated her as if she were a mindless robot, only existing to serve

his every whim. Mom couldn't even go to the store without asking Dad for permission. He stayed silent except to boss her around. She did all the dirty work while he sat on his couch and read the paper. He wouldn't let her go to church most of the time, and he complained if she quietly read the Bible. I have a hard time respecting my mom for being so stupid, and I don't respect my dad at all."

I carefully explained how the devil tries hard to pervert Christian truth, and he's done a great job with the subject of submission. In far too many churches the joy of biblical submission has been confused and twisted to mean that a wife should act as if she were a mindless doormat or a slave. Husbands have refused to talk things over with their wives, believing it was "God's will" for them to make every decision. Unbiblical submission became a handy tool for men to make their wives "shut up."

I asked this woman to come to my session for wives and see if I was doing anything to give anyone the idea that her dad had been right in the way he had treated her mother. She did come to the meeting and hugged me afterward. She said, "Oh, how I wish my mom and dad could have heard what you said today! It would have been so great to watch how this would have changed them—and me!"

It's not at all surprising that radical women's lib is gaining ground in many churches. It is a natural reaction to the devil's form of teaching on submission. Many women are vowing never to be dependent on anyone; they'll take care of themselves and be their own persons. But radical independence is not the way to avoid being stepped on. Freedom from pain begins by realizing each of us—male and female—needs Jesus Christ (see John 14:6), by learning to trust the love (see John 3:16-17) and wisdom of God (see Is. 55:8-9). As we fellowship with God, we can fellowship with each other (see 1 John 1:5-7).

Headship gives a husband the responsibility of loving and caring for his wife and family, always building in them a sense of dignity, self-respect and love for Jesus Christ. Submission gives a wife the responsibility to cooperate with her husband, encourage him and let him know she loves him even when he isn't perfect (because no human is). When both the husband and wife work together in this way the whole family will be thrilled with the results.

What Is Biblical Submission?

A Kentucky farmer defined *horse sense* as "stable thinking coupled with the ability to say nay." And that's not a bad definition for biblical submission. The "stable thinking" is a wife's ability to trust God through her husband, as she continually prays. The "ability to say nay" is the protection God always gives her to keep her from sin.

In an earlier chapter we gave a definition for biblical submission. Remember? *Submission* is "an attitude of love that *wants* to cooperate."

Note that submission is an attitude; obedience is an action.

A little boy went riding in a convertible with his dad and kept standing up to get the feel of the wind. But his dad, concerned for his son's safety, kept telling the boy to sit down. Finally, because the boy just wouldn't sit, the father said, "If you don't sit down I'm going to spank you!" The boy sat. But three minutes later the boy sighed, "My bottom's sitting. But my mind is standing up!" See, that little boy was obedient, but he was not submitted; he did not want to cooperate.

Submission to Sin? No

Colossians 3:18 makes it clear that a wife is never to sin in the name of submission: "Wives, be subject to your husbands, as is fitting in the Lord." Sin never will be "fitting in the Lord."

A woman named Sapphira paid a high price for her disobedience. God struck her dead *because* she submitted to her husband and joined him in sinning (see Acts 5:1-10). Both dropped dead on the spot. Sin is never worth that price.

Sin can't ever be "legislated" into being right. God's laws (His divine principles in the Bible) are to be obeyed whether or not they agree with man's religious or governmental laws. The real Supreme Court is not in Washington, D.C., but in heaven (see Rom. 14:12).

Peter and John refused to obey religious laws contrary to their Lord's directions even when those laws came from the highest religious authorities recognized by the government of that time (see Acts 4).

From time to time someone will ask me about 1 Peter 3:6, which refers to Abraham's wife, Sarah, obeying him, sinning by twice pretending to be his sister and risking sexual immorality. But anyone looking for illustrations proving the mercy of God needs only to follow the biblical account of Abraham and Sarah. Though this married couple ended up listed in the great Hebrews 11 Hall of Faith, they didn't always move in faith. The truth is they learned to trust God's promises, but it took them time to learn.

For example, Abram (later Abraham) twice let his wife, Sarai (later Sarah), be taken into other men's harems (see Gen. 12:10-20; 20:1-18). In explaining to the king of Gerar why he'd gambled his wife like that, he blamed God. In Genesis 20:13 Abraham said, "God caused me to wander...." The Hebrew verb Abraham used was *taah,* which means "to go astray, to cause to sin." But God never leads anyone to sin (see James 1:13). Either Abraham thought he was being led by God but missed His guidance altogether, or Abraham was frustrated and passing the buck. Whatever the reason, God knew Abraham's heart (see Gen. 18:19). He also knew he was human and, like even the best-intentioned of us, made mistakes. How marvelous and awesome is the love and mercy of our God.

It may help to know that a new wife in a harem didn't go to bed with a king for at least one year (see Esth. 2:12). Traditionally, the first half of the year in a harem was spent having the smells of the world scrubbed off. The second half of the year was spent being perfumed to the particular odor the king's nose liked best!

Sarah never entered into sin on her husband's behalf. She is no example of wife-swapping. Had God not intervened, and had she been summoned to the bed-chambers of Pharaoh or the king, she would have had to stop the situation from proceeding further. The Bible forbids any sin in the name of submission. God moved supernaturally twice to stop the situation before it could go too far. Though Abraham may be accused of situational ethics with two dreadful decisions, God, through Sarah, shows that situational ethics is never the answer. God is the answer. Second Chronicles 16:9 says, "For the eyes of the Lord move to and fro throughout the earth that He may strongly support those whose heart is completely His." God saw Sarah's dilemma and her loving attitude of obedience to her husband and "strongly supported" Sarah, "whose heart was completely His."

Let's look at 1 Peter 3:6: "Thus Sarah obeyed Abraham, calling him lord, and you have become her children if you do what is right without being frightened by any fear.'' Only the ignorant or carnal mind would suggest that Peter was commending Sarah's obedience to Abraham during these episodes in the harem. God condemns wife-swapping (see Heb. 13:4). Again, "Let no one say when he is tempted, 'I am being tempted by God'; for God cannot be tempted by evil, and He Himself does not tempt anyone" (James 1:13). Then what is Peter commending? He is praising any wife who, in spite of knowing the many mistakes her husband makes, will trust her husband and continue to submit to him in any area that is not sinful.

There are wives who feel they're "submitting" to God by simply staying in their marriages with gritted teeth. Like the little boy in the convertible, their bottoms are sitting, but their minds are standing up! They're not trying to love their husbands or be real wives to them. In fact, they've emotionally divorced their husbands. But emotional divorce is sin and breaks every rule of God regarding marriage. "Little children, let us not love with word or with tongue, but in deed and truth" (1 John 3:18).

Sometimes I'm asked, "What if my husband doesn't deserve my cooperation?" But cooperation isn't necessary because it's "deserved," but because he, functioning rightly (see Eph. 5:25) or wrongly (see 1 Peter 3:1) except in matters of sin, is the "head." A wife must be in order herself to function in the "authority" the Lord has provided her (see 1 Cor. 11:3).

Take the example of another authority, a policeman. Suppose you were speeding, and a policeman stopped you and wrote you a ticket. But as he was writing the ticket you discovered this particular policeman had a lousy personality. What should you do if you don't like his personality? Should you tear up the ticket? You'd better not! His authority isn't granted him because of his personality but because of who he is. The same truth equally applies to the husband-wife relationship.

You may not always feel like following your husband's lead. One pastor's wife, whose husband had moved the household to a city where she absolutely did not want to live, eventually found the peace that comes from surrendering her will. She wrote me about it.

For three years in this new city she resisted in resentment, which built up in her until she asked God to take her life. At that moment Romans 12:1 came to her mind: We are to present ourselves as "living sacrifices." As she surrendered her will to Jesus Christ, Lord of her life with no reservations, she was overwhelmed with peace. "From that day," she wrote, "this place became home. I know Christ led us here through my husband."

Sometimes we husbands really do have God's will in mind, even when it might not seem like it to you. I feel this was the case when I once told Arlyne not to serve on a church committee that would have tied her up most Friday nights. When I have a Friday night free, I need to be with my wife. Our kids were then in elementary school, and Friday night was the one night of the school-year week when they were able to stay up late and sleep in the next morning. The church committee would have been fine, but our marriage and family in Christ came first.

There's a War On!

The Greek word for *subject* or *submit, hupotasso,* is used forty-four times in fourteen books of the New Testament. It is a military term meaning "to place in proper order," indicating the arrangement of troops for moving into battle. Ephesians 6:12 explains our battle: "For our struggle is not against flesh and blood." Have you been thinking that your spouse is your enemy and that your fight is against a human being? Ephesians 6:12 continues, "but [our struggle is] against the rulers, against the powers, against the world forces of this darkness, against the spiritual forces of wickedness in the heavenly places."

There *is* a war on. To win this war a husband and wife must both place themselves in the right order. A husband must place himself directly under the loving command of Jesus Christ, and a wife must place herself under the loving command of her husband (1 Cor. 11:3). "Spiritual warfare" means walking in the full armor of God described in Ephesians 6, walking in truth and righteousness, keeping the peace, believing God in spite of whatever flaming missiles the devil throws at them, keeping their minds constantly sharpened by the Word of God and praying "at all times in the Spirit," for themselves and for others. Want some good news while you're doing this? I've read the last pages of the Bible, and you've already won if you just keep on keeping on!

> Therefore, since we have so great a cloud of witnesses surrounding us, let us also lay aside every encumbrance, and the sin which

so easily entangles us, and let us run with endurance the race that is set before us, fixing our eyes on Jesus, the author and perfecter of faith, who for the joy set before Him endured the cross, despising the shame, and has sat down at the right hand of the throne of God. For consider Him who has endured such hostility by sinners against Himself, so that you may not grow weary and lose heart (Heb. 12:1-3).

THE TRUE CHRISTIAN IS A PERSON WHO IS RIGHT-SIDE-UP IN A WORLD THAT IS UPSIDE DOWN!

Questions for Reflection and Discussion

1. Study Matthew 16:24-25 and 1 Peter 5:6-7 in light of this chapter on submission. According to 1 Peter 5:6, what will the Lord do for any wife who biblically submits to her husband over a long period of time? Write a paraphrase of 1 Peter 5:6.

2. List the two special purposes of a wife according to Genesis 2:18. Under each purpose list at least four ways you are doing this.

3. Reread the section called "The Titus Five"—attributes older wives are to teach younger wives. How successfully are these attributes being taught a) in your society? b) in your schools c) in your church? d) in your home? Get in a private place before God and ask Him alone to show you how you are doing in each of these areas. Wherever He indicates you are weak, pray for guidance: What should you do to gain new strength in this area? Have a pad of paper with you and write down what you believe He tells you to do. Be sure His answers agree with His written Word, the Bible.

4. Consider the statement, "No one can sin and biblically submit at the same time." Why not? Consider Colossians 3:18 and Acts 1:1-10 in formulating your written answer.

5. Read 1 Peter 3:6. Reread the section in this past chapter concerning Abraham and Sarah and read Genesis 12:10-20; 20:1-18. How do we know this is not a direction from God to wife-swap, even if your husband demands it? Read Hebrews 13:4; James 1:13; and Acts 5:27-29 in formulating your answer.

Dear Ray,

   You are coming to our church a month from now. Maybe I should wait and just talk with you when you get here. But I'm so frustrated, I'm writing. It's my husband. He will not listen to me. He's got enough faults to start a thousand earthquakes. I try to help him get over some of them. I know it would make both of us a lot happier if he didn't do a lot of things he does. But he *won't listen.* He gets mad if I dare open my mouth. Divorce is out of the question because I really love the Lord. Ray, I love my husband, too. That's what hurts. If I didn't love him it would be a lot easier to cope with his shrugging me off or barking at me whenever I say anything about his need to change. I have red hair so it won't be hard to spot me if I sit in the front row, which I usually do. You'll be able to spot my husband, too. He always wears loud ties. He thinks they're "flashy." It's one of the things I'd most like to change. I'm eager for you to come. Maybe you can get through his thick noggin.

In Christian Love

*"In the same way,
you wives, be submissive
to your own husbands so
that even if any of them are
disobedient to the word, they may
be won without a word by the
behavior of their wives."*

1 Peter 3:1

TEN

Real Wife-Power

KEEPING HUSBANDS IN HOT WATER DOES NOT HELP TO MAKE THEM TENDER!

Husbands are as unique as thumbprints. And no husband is perfect. I've always chuckled over the remark made by Carole Lombard when she was married to Clark Gable: "Clark Gable is no Clark Gable at our house!"

Genesis 6:9 tells us God chose Noah to keep the world going, not because he was perfect, but because he was righteous, or headed in the right direction. That was enough to save his whole family.

Even if your husband was perfect, you might not recognize it. After all, Jesus Christ liked fish for breakfast. Do you?

Ephesians 5:24 tells all wives, "But as the church is subject to Christ, so also the wives ought to be to their husbands in everything." I know that word *everything* can blow one's mind. So I did what I knew every female reader would want me to do: I looked up the original Greek word translated here as *everything*. And I found out the Greek word means *everything!*

To help you get a grasp on what *everything* means, it may help to know that all of life can be fitted under one of three headings:

1. *Spiritual experiences.* Spiritual submission is covered in 1 Peter 3:1-6.

2. *Emotional experiences.* Emotional submission is covered in Ephesians 5:33.

3. *Physical experiences.* Physical submission is covered in 1 Corinthians 7:2-5.

In this chapter let's look at the first two areas, spiritual and emotional experiences as they relate to submission. We'll discuss the physical-sexual area of life in a later chapter.

Spiritual Submission

In the same way, you wives, be submissive to your own husbands so that even if any of them are disobedient to the word, they may be won without a word by the behavior of their wives, as they observe your chaste and respectful behavior. And let not your adornment be merely external—braiding the hair, and wearing gold jewelry, and putting on dresses; but let it be the hidden person of the heart, with the imperishable quality of a gentle and quiet spirit, which is precious in the sight of God. For in this way in former times the holy women also, who hoped in God, used to adorn themselves, being submissive to their own husbands. Thus Sarah obeyed Abraham, calling him lord, and you have become her children if you do what is right without being frightened by any fear (1 Pet. 3:1-6).

Once in a while when I read this text in a church, someone will point out that their King James Version says wives will win their husbands to God by their "conversation" (v. 1). But when the King James Version was published in 1611 the word *conversation* meant "behavior." It had nothing to do with talking, except when talking was part of the good behavior.

You may be thinking, But I *have* to tell him how I feel; I can't only pray about everything that concerns, worries, upsets or embarrasses me. You're right. We'll talk about *that* in chapter 11.

If I ask one question, you wives will know what I mean when I say that conversation doesn't work! Here's the question: Once you were married, how long did it take you to discover that no matter how long you lectured your husband about something he did do but shouldn't have, or didn't do but should have, you never seemed to get your point across?

Christian Wives With Unsaved Husbands

Imagine the problem a first-century wife faced if she chose to become a Christian. It hadn't been done before. In his book *The Letters of James and Peter,* William Barclay explains,

> For a wife to change her religion while her husband did not was unthinkable....Under Roman law a woman had no rights. In law she remained forever a child. When she was under her father she was under the patria potestas, the father's power, which gave the father the right of even life and death over her; and when she married she passed equally into the power of her husband. She was entirely subject to her husband and completely at his mercy. It is almost impossible for us to realize what life must have been like for the wife who was brave enough to become a Christian...[Peter] takes exactly the same attitude as Paul (1 Corinthians 7:13-16)....Peter does not tell the wife to preach or argue. He does not tell her to insist that there is "...no difference between...male and female...." He tells her something very simple—nothing else than to be a good wife. It is by the silent preaching of the loveliness of her life that she must break down the prejudice and hostility, and win her husband for her new Master.[1]

If Peter and Paul were men writing for their day only, we could dismiss their teaching. But the Bible was not written by men, but by the Holy Spirit through these men. "But know this first of all, that no prophecy of Scripture is a matter of one's own interpretation, for no prophecy was ever made by an act of human will, but men moved by the Holy Spirit spoke from God" (2 Pet. 1:20-21).

The situation for many women today is similar to the one described by Peter: They have come to Christ but their husbands haven't. Peter patiently tells every wife how to lead her husband to the Lord. The ways of God and the Word of God are unchangeable (see Rev. 22:18-19).

Ratbags!

One of my favorite countries is New Zealand. My wife and I picked up a term in New Zealand that has seemed perfect for certain men we've heard about or met. The term is *ratbags,* and New Zealanders use the word to describe men who treat their wives or families badly. Ratbags commit adultery or won't support their families financially or seem to delight in tormenting their wives and kids. Most ratbags don't know Christ. Some are prodigal sons still out with the pigs. A few ratbags obey God in nearly everything but have some one thing they hold back. First Peter 3:1 tells wives what to do with ratbags. The good news is wives can change them into godly men "without a word" to them. (Well, you might try an encouraging word. Talk to a man about his good traits, and he'll listen to you for hours.)

Some wife, on reading that she is to win her husband to obedience to Christ "without a word," might argue, "But I've got to straighten him out!" Another wife may answer, "But I've got to be *honest* with him!" Well, mirrors and cameras are honest, but both are often avoided. Ratbags do cause a great deal of frustration in any home. But let me ask again, has nagging worked in the past? When something doesn't work, it's time to find a better answer. First Peter 3:1 *is* the better answer.

Hands in the Pockets!

I now smile at an incident that happened in Pasadena, California, sometime during our first twelve years of marriage.

At that point Arlyne had a list that must have been at least ten miles long: things she didn't like about me. One of the things on the list was that I put my hands in my pockets. (I'm not the tallest man in the world, nor the thinnest. I didn't realize that when I stuck my hands in my pockets I looked even wider than I was. Nor did I realize that when other women looked at me my wife thought they were thinking, "That's what she picked?")

So one day as we started into a department store, Arlyne said, probably for the umpteenth time that day, "Ray, get your hands out of your pockets!" Well, I did. I took my hands out of my pockets—and dropped back behind her. Arlyne didn't notice and kept walking. I watched her walk down an aisle and go out of sight. The moment she got out of sight I plunged my hands into my pockets.

Almost any husband will react to his wife's criticism the same way I did. You see, a wife is to transform her husband without a word to him. How can she possibly do that? Through the unstoppable power of prayer.

God can get a husband's hands out of his pockets—or completely change a wife's mind so that it no longer bothers her. (That's what He did with

172

my wife on *that* subject, praise the Lord!) In truth, God can make *any* change that is needed. If a wife will tell the Lord, instead of her husband, about the thing that needs changing, she's on her way to seeing a miracle. The day a wife begins to quit nagging her husband and begins instead to confide in and trust God, her husband will begin doing things she never thought he'd do and stop doing things she never thought he'd stop. But any wife who doesn't have a deep and abiding prayer life will frustrate herself and her marriage until she does.

A listener to my "Marriage Plus" radio program wrote me her story. She wanted a sewing machine. Though it seemed a reasonable request, her husband wouldn't agree to buying one. At least twice a week for six months this wife found some way to show him she needed that machine. She cried. She nagged. They fought about it.

One day she heard me talking about giving non-vital matters to the Lord for Him to decide. She gave the sewing machine to God and promised Him she'd not mention the machine to her husband. Maybe it really was too expensive, she figured. Three months passed, and she kept her tongue. Then one day while shopping with her husband, they both saw the machine at half price. She still said nothing. After making all their other purchases, he finally said, "Honey, let's get that sewing machine too!" They did. God rewards faith (see Heb. 11:6).

Jan Teague, who ministers to women in Melbourne, Australia, says, "We wives must spend less time telling our husbands about God and more time telling God about our husbands. Then we will see the change!"

Worrying is like being in a rocking chair. It gives you something to do, but it doesn't get you anywhere. A problem not worth praying about isn't worth worrying about. God will move heaven and earth when a wife prays, believing Him (see John 15:7).

"Holier Than Thou"

In the days when I was "churched," before I repented and really gave my life to Jesus Christ, I had what I considered a sure-fire Christian creed: "I don't smoke, I don't chew. And I don't go with the girls who do!" Then one day my dog put his head right in my lap, and the silliest thought went through my mind: My dog doesn't smoke. My dog doesn't chew. And I couldn't think of one girl my dog had gone with who did! My dog and I were equally "righteous."

That's what Isaiah meant when he said, "For all of us have become like one who is unclean, and all our righteous deeds are like a filthy garment" (Is. 64:6). Or, as the New Testament tells us, "But now apart from the Law the righteousness of God has been manifested...even the righteousness of God through faith in Jesus Christ for all those who believe; for there is no distinction; for all have sinned and fall short of the glory of God" (Rom 3:21-23). If our own righteousness could have saved us, Jesus Christ would never have had to die for us. "Our righteous deeds are like a filthy garment."

Yet there is a righteousness that isn't filthy at all. Romans 4:3 (referring to Genesis 15:6) says, "And Abraham believed God, and it was reckoned to him as righteousness." *Believing God* gives you a "clean" righteousness. I ask every wife, "Do you believe God? Do you believe He is big enough to change your husband where your husband really needs changing? Are you willing to trust God rather than yourself to bring about the change in him? Are you willing to act upon the Word of God instead of upon your feelings to see a miracle in your husband or a change important to the joy of both of you?" If you are willing, God will count that as "clean" righteousness in you and begin immediately to do the changing. Just keep "working together" with Jesus Christ (2 Cor. 6:1), be obedient to God's Word, and you'll see it. Small wonder the apostle Paul, in speaking of the love of Christ, stopped and said, "Now to Him who is able to do exceeding abundantly beyond all that we ask or think, according to the power that works within us, to Him be the glory in the church and in Christ Jesus to all generations forever and ever. Amen" (Eph. 3:20-21).

Let's continue looking at 1 Peter 3:1-6. Here's verse 2: Husbands may be won to the Lord "...as they observe your chaste and respectful behavior."

In the church too many people, instead of letting their lights shine, spend their time trying to put out other people's lights! Peter deals with this problem, saying a wife will bring her rebellious husband to obey Christ and God's Word as he sees his wife's "chaste" and "respectful behavior."

The word translated *chaste* means "consecrated" or "reserved." Peter is saying a wife's actions must show she is "consecrated to" or "reserved for" her husband. The wife is never to make her husband jealous. And that makes the other key adjective in 1 Peter 3:2 very significant: "respectful" or "reverential." He needs her to make him feel he is the most important human in her life.

A wife who is born again after her marriage is likely to dig deeper and deeper into the things of the Lord, wanting to learn everything she can about the Lord and do everything she can for Him. But her unsaved husband will not share her zeal. "But a natural [carnal] man does not accept the things of the Spirit of God; for they are foolishness to him, and he cannot understand them, because they are spiritually appraised" (1 Cor. 2:14). In fact, he well may be antagonistic toward God and anything representing God "...because the mind set on the flesh is hostile toward God; for it does not subject itself to the law of God, for it is not even able to do so" (Rom. 8:7). A wife who expects her unsaved husband to be thrilled at something the Lord has done is asking too much of him. An unsaved mind "is not even able to do so." In fact, if her unsaved husband begins to watch the "700 Club" with any interest at all, the wife had better accept that as a sign from heaven: Something good may be about to happen. (Handle with prayer.)

A problem can arise when the wife, hungry for God, gets heavily involved with the things of God, including church activities, and starts neglecting her husband. As she gets busier and busier, he grows angrier and angrier. She is often gone when he feels he needs her; when she's home, she keeps trying to lead him to Christ by telling him how much she "loves Jesus." She talks on and on about Jesus. Jesus is so wonderful. Jesus takes care of her. Jesus blesses her. She hangs Jesus' picture in the bathroom where her husband is sure to see it. Or, at night, thinking herself spiritual, she props up her pillow, reads her Bible and avoids having sex with her unspiritual husband. And she wonders why he avoids Jesus Christ, Christianity, church and her.

Quite unthinkingly, she isn't drawing her husband to Jesus Christ. She is driving him away. The husband is silently growing jealous of Christ. It is as if his wife had a new lover, worst of all, an invisible one! If the husband could see this new contender for his wife's love, he very well might fight him. But how does a husband fight Jesus Christ? He can only retreat, because his wife obviously loves Christ more than she does him.

175

Peter says, "Stop it, wife! You give your open reverence to your husband. Lavish your love on him. Then he won't be afraid to love the Lord."

Adorned With Gentleness

Peter continues:

> And let not your adornment be merely external—braiding the hair, and wearing gold jewelry, or putting on dresses; but let it be the hidden person of the heart, with the imperishable quality of a gentle and quiet spirit, which is precious in the sight of God (1 Pet. 3:3-4).

Some say verse 3 means that a woman should wear no make-up or jewelry. But that interpretation drawn out would mean that a woman should wear no clothes!

In *The Letters of James and Peter,* William Barclay again brings Peter's meaning into focus when he comments concerning the first-century attitude toward women who spent staggeringly large sums of money on clothing and jewelry: "Undue interest in self-adornment was then, as it still is, a sign that the person who indulged in it had no greater things to occupy her mind."[2]

"The hidden person of the heart" is the human spirit with the Holy Spirit inside (see 2 Cor. 4:16; Rom. 7:22; Eph. 3:16; 4:24; et al.). A woman who trusts God and stays quiet and loving when it seems she has every right to holler is precious to God and powerful! First Peter 3:5 continues: "For in this way in former times the holy women also, who hoped in God, used to adorn themselves, being submissive to their own husbands."

We may be living in modern days, but God is telling every Christian to live with the highest principles of former times. Notice the words "hoped in God." When a wife puts her hope in God and trusts Him, He will move heaven and earth to bring her husband into obedience to His Word.

No Need to Fear

First Peter 3:6: "Thus Sarah obeyed Abraham, calling him lord, and you have become her children if you do what is right without being frightened by any fear."

We've looked at this verse previously. In short, Sarah learned to trust God through Abraham. The lessons that led to her trusting him came over many hard years. But God was pleased with this woman.

Notice: "do what is right." Obey the Lord. Sarah made mistakes. Some of them were whoppers (see Gen. 16:1-6). But falling down doesn't make a failure. Staying down does.

If you do what is right, don't be "frightened by any fear." Don't say, "Yes, but what if he told me to...(your worst possible fear)?" Remember, we lie to God when we pray if we don't rely on God after we pray!

Sometimes a fear flies away as you name the worst thing that could possibly happen and then recognize it wouldn't be so bad after all—especially if the alternative is to take matters into your own hands and lose the blessings of both God and your husband.

Sometimes allowing a husband to fail will cause him to turn to God. Never say, "If I don't do it, it won't get done!" If it is your husband's responsibility, and he hasn't directly asked you to do it, then it won't be done right even if it does get done. There are exceptions, of course, especially if a husband has directly asked his wife to help him in any matter that isn't sinful. In such a case, pray earnestly while submitting, as Sarah must have done many times (since she received such a strong commendation from God), and the Lord can speak to your husband and show him why he needs to relieve you of the task or bless you thoroughly as you fulfill your assignment.

First Peter 3:1-6 Summarized

1. God wants your husband more than you do. Jesus Christ died for him. If you'll cooperate with the Lord, He'll get the job done.

2. Therefore be in subjection, deliberately taking second place in your marriage. "Humble yourselves, therefore, under the mighty hand of God, that He may exalt you at the proper time" (1 Pet. 5:6).

3. Stay silent rather than criticize. Never preach at him. If he is lost, share with him only the miracles you are discovering as a Christian. If he tells you to stop even that, tell God on him (see 1 Pet. 5:6-7).

4. Let Christ be seen in your spirit. Continuously pour love on your husband (see Rom 12:14). Live so as to please Jesus (see Col. 3:23-24).

5. Maintain a "meek and quiet spirit" (1 Pet. 3:4, KJV). But don't

confuse meekness with weakness. Meekness has been beautifully described as "great strength under God's control." It is willing submission to the will of God. Let me paraphrase 1 Pet. 5:6: Humble yourself before your husband, and in due season you will be exalted.

Corrie ten Boom once said, "When a train goes through a tunnel and it gets dark, you don't throw away your ticket and jump off. You sit still and trust the engineer!"

Emotional (or Mental) Submission

"Let the wife see that she respects and reverences her husband—that she notices him, regards him, honors him, prefers him, venerates and esteems him; and that she defers to him, praises him, and loves and admires him exceedingly" (Eph. 5:33, Amplified).

The Bible is always right on the bull's eye. What does a husband need most of all? Respect. As Mae West once said, "Man ain't everything. But they're the best opposite sex we've got!"

I'm a real admirer of our first lady, the no-nonsense but rib-tickling Barbara Bush. No wonder our president has such a happy smile. She always has just the right comment. When the president was attacked by some of the press for not liking broccoli, she said, "My husband is never going to eat broccoli. Accepting that fact is one of the reasons we've stayed married forty-five years." That is godly wisdom.

There is no sin in not eating broccoli. As President Bush himself said, "Let the rest of the nation eat broccoli." And there is no sin in squeezing the toothpaste from the middle or the end of the tube.

Barbara let George be George, respecting him for who he is.

A lot of annoying (though not necessarily sinful) habits come to us as part of our cultural background. Some people are very quiet. Others are loud (like me). Personal quirks learned when we were young become habits that are as hard to stop as a sneeze. When we relax—or tense up—we do certain things, which we wish we didn't do. The "accuser of our brethren" (Rev. 12:10) stands by to let us know what a jerk we are. When a wife joins the devil in telling her husband he's a failure, he's sure no man in the world is as terrible as he is and/or no woman in the world is as terrible as she is. Either way it hurts the marriage terribly.

Your husband may have more good qualities than you think. Recently a wife came to me to say that she was heartbroken over her husband's unspirituality. She proceeded to tell me how her husband fell asleep during sermons and that he objected to studying the Bible with her every night. Later the pastor of their church pointed out this same man. The pastor, not knowing this man's wife had spoken to me, said, "I thank God for that man every day. He's absolutely dependable. If I need a leak in the baptistry repaired or a sound system put in or my car fixed, he'll work on it as long as it takes without any complaint. I'm about to appoint him as a deacon." You see, his wife didn't have an unspiritual husband. She just didn't understand that she had a tired one; she was married to a "server," according to Romans 12:7.

Nothing I've just written is a cop-out for a husband. Sir, you've got to work at blessing your wife just as she needs to work at blessing you.

Find Out Who He Is

I sometimes find that husbands and wives don't know each other very well. Ask your husband to write down a list of things he likes to do. And you write a list also. You may discover some surprises.

Dear Ray,

A month ago you were in our church and did the Marriage Plus Seminar. A month ago I was thinking so hard about wanting a divorce that I didn't plan to come to your seminar. I went because my best friend insisted. Am I glad! For ten years I regretted marrying my husband. I thought we had nothing in common. Guess what? I don't believe that anymore. You told us to write down ten things we liked about our husbands. I struggled with writing four. Then my husband and I talked—like we've never talked before. I found out he used to collect stamps when he was a kid. He'd never told me that. I used to collect stamps when I was a girl too. We had *that* in common! He liked going to the ballet when he was a kid! I almost fell over. Him? The ballet? We went to a ballet that Saturday night. I love ballets. We'd just never shared that kind of information before. Well, I could go on and tell you more. But please, Ray, receive my real thanks for telling me to accept my husband "just as he is without one plea." I have and I will. We have a lot in common!

Enjoy Him

As your husband sees you want to get to know him and respect who he is, he will start enjoying your company. One wife told me how glad she was to find her husband was interested in auto races. She had gone to and enjoyed a few races with her brother when she was in high school. When she and her husband started to make their list together, he mentioned liking the races. She picked up on it, and now they go often.

But what if you hate auto races and he loves them? In *Help! I'm a Pastor's Wife* Arlyne talked about her feelings toward baseball:

> [Ray] loves going to baseball games. I, on the other hand, find them boring unless there's a lot of hitting and the score is in the neighborhood of 25 to 23—not too likely if you're watching Major League games. I go anyway and look for the good plays, watch people, enjoy the outdoors and have a hot dog. The game may not be fun, but being with Ray is.

Being with a good sport is fun for me too. All of our kids, like me, are big baseball fanatics. Yea, Dodgers!

By the way, if your husband is a sports nut and wishes you were too, show your respect for him by finding out what you can about the players on his favorite team. One thing Arlyne and I did enjoy together, even during those first bad years of marriage, was listening to Dodger games over the radio. That's because radio announcer Vin Scully made the game interesting for Arlyne. He not only called the plays, he gave background information on the players: One guy's mother knitted his socks; another player played the clarinet....To Arlyne that made the players real people.

It makes sense: If the right side of the brain loves relationships, the more personal the athlete seems the more apt you will be to enjoy his role in a game.

Walk toward your husband, and he will walk toward you.

Wives, take an interest in learning about your husband's work, even though it may not naturally interest or excite you. I understand Thomas Edison's wife told him, "I don't know what you're doing, Tom, but I can't sleep with that light on!"

Forgive Him

I've said it before. I'll say it again. Your husband won't be perfect, and respect calls for forgiveness.

It is a heavy truth that if we don't forgive, the Lord won't forgive us. But that's exactly what Matthew 6:14-15 tells us. Mark Twain said, "Forgiveness is the perfume a flower gives off when somebody steps on it." Forgiveness is an essential life ingredient in any marriage that wants to keep love in it.

For years I've treasured the story told by Shelley Bassett about what her grandmother told the guests at her grandmother's golden wedding celebration. Her grandma said, "On my wedding day, I decided to make a list of ten of my husband's faults which, for the sake of our marriage, I would overlook." A guest at the party asked what some of the overlooked faults were. Shelley's grandmother said, "To tell you the truth, my dear, I never did get around to listing them. But whenever my husband did something that made me hopping mad, I would say to myself, 'Lucky for him that's one of the ten!' "

My darlin' Arlyne and I have a lot of fun together. But I have a lot of faults. For example, I have forgotten both Arlyne's birthday and our anniversary. What do you suppose she did about that? Let me quote her again from a chapter in *Help! I'm a Pastor's Wife*:

> I took Ray to San Francisco to celebrate our anniversary on spare change I had been putting away for several months. He knew nothing about my little hoard and enjoyed the evening all the more because we normally would not have been able to afford it. I planned the anniversary outing to San Francisco—paid for with nickels, dimes and quarters—because I *knew* Ray had forgotten the date.
>
> The old Arlyne would have fumed over his thoughtlessness and made him miserable for forgetting such an important day. The new one simply organized an exciting night out for her husband.

Love covers up the lapses in each other. It was when I decided not to place blame or feel sorry for myself, but to concentrate on loving Ray, and vice versa, that great joy was released to both of us. That evening after dinner, I presented Ray with a little plastic bag tied with a bright red ribbon and a tag that read, "Happy Anniversary." When he opened it, he found all of the change I had collected and an advertisement for a show being performed in the city by our favorite male vocalist. He couldn't have been more surprised or more pleased. We dropped our son Tim at the home of a friend and scooted off to our anniversary celebration—one of the best we've ever had.

It sure was! But, oh, how she could have spoiled that anniversary by showing me disrespect. She had every "right" to be angry, but she chose not to be angry. See why I call her my darlin' Arlyne?

By the way, I did remember her birthday last year. I took her to Alcatraz! She loved it!

A Last Word

I don't mean to be saying that a wife is to stay silent over something important to her. The way something is said will usually make all the difference in the world. Let's look at a few proverbs.

"A constant dripping on a rainy day and a cranky woman are much alike! You can no more stop her complaints than you can stop the wind or hold onto anything with oil-slick hands" (Prov. 27:15-16, LB).

"It is better to live in the corner of an attic than with a crabby woman in a lovely home" (Prov. 21:9, LB).

"Better to live in the desert than with a quarrelsome, complaining woman" (Prov. 21:19, LB).

"A worthy wife is her husband's joy and crown; the other kind corrodes his strength and tears down everything he does" (Prov. 12:4, LB).

"Timely advice is as lovely as golden apples in a silver basket" (Prov. 25:11, LB). Can't you just picture that silver basket and those golden apples? Wow, what a magnificent sight! It's elegant. There's nothing cheap or brassy about it. That's how you *can* appear to your husband when you say something to him to help him gain a new light in an area that might otherwise cause problems.

Arlyne says she used to expect me to be able to read her mind. "When he couldn't, my dissatisfaction became 'his fault,' not mine. But eventually, with the Lord's help, and Ray's encouragement, I took more responsibility for my feelings and became more transparent and less afraid to express my needs." I'm *so glad* to hear what Arlyne is feeling, needing, hoping to have me do, because I know she isn't going to attack me. Ladies, share with your man—in love. Guys, listen to your woman. Love each other.

Be careful for the tone of your voice, the volume, the look on your face, body language, etc. Because if he feels you don't have respect for him when you say it, you'll lose. In fact, making him feel like a wimp will make it all the harder for you to respect him. One reason some men avoid their wives sexually is because of the subconscious feeling that they don't want to make love to their mothers!

Read the coming chapter on communication several times. Arguing with a husband is just going to keep the anger stirred, and both of you will stay frustrated. If it's really important, and he won't hear you after you've lovingly told him something, tell God!

The more important the issue is to you, the more you need to pray about it. The more you let God know how much what you're carrying emotionally hurts, the more quickly God will move on your behalf.

Jesus Christ promised, "If you abide in Me, and My words abide in you, ask whatever you wish, and it shall be done for you" (John 15:7). Expect a miracle (see Heb. 11:1; Ps. 50:15), but wait on God's perfect timing (see Luke 18:1). He might be doing something in *you* first (see James 1:2-4).

Trusting God by telling Him what you would otherwise say to your husband will bring changes you won't see happen any other way.

In this chapter for wives, I'll let Arlyne have the last word: "If you think Ray is the one who gives me peace of mind, you're mistaken. I love Ray. I love being Ray's wife. But it is Jesus Christ who gives me peace and satisfies my deepest needs. Yet Christ never shuts Ray out, but He blesses Ray through me."

TRUE LOVE DOESN'T HAVE A HAPPY ENDING.
TRUE LOVE DOESN'T HAVE AN ENDING!

Questions for Reflection and Discussion

1. First Peter 3:1-6 describes how a wife can attract an unsaved or rebellious Christian husband to the Lord. Write down the key instructions in that passage. Now read Galatians 5:22-23 and list the fruit of the Spirit. Which fruit is needed to carry out each of the instructions listed in 1 Peter 3:1-6?

2. Read 1 Peter 3:1; John 15:7; and Mark 11:24. Which do you, as a wife, believe will accomplish more: prayer or your instructions and corrections? Tell why.

3. Suppose a wife wrote you that she didn't feel her husband deserved her cooperation. Answer her letter by writing another letter. Read 1 Peter 3:1; 1 Corinthians 7:12-14; Matthew 5:44-46; and Romans 12:17-21 to help you formulate your answer to her.

4. Rewrite Proverbs 12:4 in your own words. Read Proverbs 27:15-16; Proverbs 21:9; Proverbs 21:19; and Ephesians 4:29 in formulating your paraphrase.

Dear Ray,

I am divorced. I came to your seminar to see what I did wrong. I expected to come away with a load of condemnation. Instead, I came away only grieving that I'd never heard those things you shared from the Bible before. I know it would have saved my marriage. Veronica is a lovely woman. We were married eight years. I got her pregnant and married her. We were just out of high school. We never talked. We made love on dates, and that didn't require talk. We went to movies, and that didn't require talk. So for eight years I mumbled my way through our marriage. When Veronica tried to talk to me, I'd just cut her off. I watched a lot of television. She watched it for a while, but she got tired of not talking then, either. Now she's gone. I got saved at your seminar, Ray. Now, with your teaching and the Holy Spirit inside me, I think I could talk to Veronica. But she's gone. I sure miss her. There's nobody to talk with now at home. Of course, I talk to God. Wish you were here. Maybe we could talk.

Learned Too Late

"But speaking the truth in love, we are to grow up in all aspects into Him, who is the head, even Christ."

Ephesians 4:15

ELEVEN

Two, Four, Six, Eight— Communicate!

WHETHER YOU ARE ON THE ROAD OR IN AN ARGUMENT, WHEN YOU BEGIN TO SEE RED, STOP!

Marriage is the complete upheaval of the settled routines of two adults who, until marriage, could be as selfish as they chose to be without too much effect—except lost friends!

I remind every single person who attends my Singles Plus seminar, "You both gain and lose a lot of things when you get married. You gain a partner who will work with you (if you're marrying a Christian) and help you be more than you could ever be without that person. But you lose the ability to do everything on your own, do only what you want to do, eat only what you want to eat, sleep in if you don't want to get up, watch only the TV programs you want to see, quit a job if you don't like it, move to another town if you prefer or join the circus. In short, you lose the ability to be selfish without paying a horrible price."

To anyone reading the above statement who says, "But if the marriage doesn't work out, I can always get a divorce," Someone has said that divorce is "like a shoot-out between Siamese twins." No matter what happens, both partners become casualties. Divorced people generally die younger than those who stay married.

A husband reading this book has probably already read the chapter called "Real Wife-Power." Since 1 Peter 3:1 tells wives to win their husbands to Christ "without a word" to them, you might think that wives should be the silent partners in marriage. But, as the Greek philosopher Socrates wrote, "Is there anyone to whom you entrust more serious matters than your wife? And is there anyone to whom you talk less?"

Nowhere does the Bible say a wife should remain the silent partner. Any husband who thinks he's proved he's the boss in the family because his wife never says anything is "cruising for a bruising." One of these days all the pressure that silence is building within her is going to explode. You may spend the rest of your life trying to pick up the shattered pieces of your marriage.

Yes, prayer will move the unmovable (see Mark 11:23-24) and make possible the impossible (see Mark 9:23). But God has given all men and women free will. You can choose to rebel against God and your spouse—and suffer the consequences.

Jesus Christ said this about free will, "How often I wanted to gather your children together...and you were unwilling" (Matt. 23:37). God will not turn a husband into a robot or a wife into a wind-up doll to make either obey Him. But the person who lives for self alone usually dies the same way. As C.S. Lewis so beautifully wrote, "Either you tell God 'Thy will be done' while you are still alive. Or, on judgment day, God will say to you, 'thy will be done.' "

Much of what I'm going to say in this chapter is for husbands because we guys are meant to be the head of our homes. We are also responsible for the life of each person in our immediate family, especially those who live under our roof. The buck stops with us. Any family mistakes reflect on us and on how we have led the family. The "wife's fault" isn't the wife's fault but the husband's fault if he's done nothing in God to change what led to her fault or mistake or sin. Adam could have stopped Eve from eating the fruit that made the whole world sick. He could have said, "Wait a minute!" when she added to God's Word, saying they couldn't even touch the fruit (see Gen. 3:2-3). But Adam's silence was deadly. Why didn't he communicate the truth to her? There's no acceptable excuse for his not doing it—nor for you.

Jesus Christ is subject to the Father (see John 8:28-29) in every way and always will be (see 1 Cor. 15:28). But Jesus Christ could always pray to His Father (see Matt. 14:23; Mark 1:35; Luke 22:44; 23:34). A wife is to be subject to her husband in every way and always will be. But she

should always be allowed to communicate with her husband.
Philippians 2:1-4 tells all Christians everywhere:

> If therefore there is any encouragement in Christ, if there is any
> consolation of love, if there is any fellowship of the Spirit, if any
> affection and compassion, make my joy complete by being of the
> same mind, maintaining the same love, united in spirit, intent on
> one purpose. Do nothing from selfishness or empty conceit, but
> with humility of mind *let each of you regard one another as more
> important than himself;* do not merely look out for your own
> personal interests, but also for the interests of others (italics mine).

Choking down anger and frustration because you can't say something
to your spouse leaves you smoldering in resentment. Have you ever
had a suggestion that you felt would improve your job situation? But you
knew your boss would never let you say it? Remember how frustrated
you were? Well, that's what happens when a wife can't say something
to her husband.

It's right to discuss with each other desires, dreams, wants, goals and
anything else that concerns either of you. You need to communicate—not
just talk. The dictionary defines *to talk* as "to utter words." To *communicate* means "to transfer thoughts." In fact, *communication* involves
a two-sided, stimulating conversation—but not an argument. (So "pass
the cornflakes" is not considered communication.)

Most conversations between a Christian husband and wife will be
pleasant. Even when one of them is tense over something, they will try
to "[speak] the truth in love" (Eph. 4:15). Any spouse who doesn't speak
in love will weaken the marital relationship. Most often, the more arguments
you "win," the further apart you'll stand. There are usually two sides
to an argument, but no end!

In even the most Christ-centered marriages a husband and wife will not
always agree. I've never met a family that could fully agree on which car
window should be open—and how far. If someone does not agree with
you, that person is not necessarily crazy, dumb, ugly or wrong. To disagree
is one thing. To be disagreeable is a whole different thing. A disagreement never has to become an argument. The only right way to settle a
disagreement is to determine what's right, not who's right.

Proverbs 17:14 (LB) warns, "It is hard to stop a quarrel once it starts, so don't let it begin." If you disagree, talk the issue through in a friendly, thoughtful manner.

"To draw back from a dispute is honourable; it is the fool who bears his teeth" (Prov. 20:3, NEB). Hot words never result in cool thinking.

Many children and teenagers live in hurt and terror because of the parental arguments they hear and see. There was no excuse for what Arlyne and I were doing to our son, who was developing an ulcer on our account. Divorce is not the answer. Once again, as in all things, Jesus Christ and God's Word are the answer.

May these specific points on good communication increase the joy of your marriage, as they have mine.

Decide You Will Communicate

Admittedly, this is a real challenge to the ordinary man. It seems that communication by talking is a right-brained activity. Communication by sounds is left-brained.

Observe a group of four-year-olds. A group of girls will generally be talking. If a girl can't find friends to talk to, she'll talk with her doll or herself. But boys? They'll be down on the floor with toy cars making lots of sounds: Brooooooom! Brooooooom! Brooooooom! WOMBAM! Eeeeeeeeeeeep!

Add thirty years to the ages: A married man comes home and still makes sounds. When his wife wants to communicate, he's apt to say, "Uh-huh. Mmmmmmmmmm. Yep. Uh-huh."

Experts who study the brain differences in human males and females say men are comfortable using thousands of words less a day than women do. A lot of jokes are made about this, but communication is not a laughing matter. It is essential to a great marriage.

Locked inside the amazing brain of your honey, guys, is a very active right side that loves details. Remember how well her memory works? (Or can't you remember that far back in this book?) That left side of your brain (which does need to get more in touch with the right side) wants just the main facts. In fact, the main fact is all it wants. It generally goes to sleep on details.

Want your wife to love you even more, husband? Learn to listen to her details. Let her present life to you in technicolor, not just black and white. Learn to appreciate all the vitality she brings to ordinary experiences.

Want your husband to love you even more, wife? Let him get in a few words too. Learn to ask him questions, especially if they are related to facts. Let him give you just the facts, ma'am. Don't put him on the spot, but when you are with friends, ask him to tell an experience you've both shared and enjoyed (even if you could tell it better). Draw him out as you would try to do with any good friend.

Beware of being "newspaper reporters" with each other. If your spouse is telling a story and says, "Yes, we went down the street three blocks," don't interrupt and say, "No, no, no, it was four blocks." Nobody cares how many blocks it was. There's not going to be a test on the number of blocks when the conversation is finished. But being contradicted like that is sure to make a spouse angry.

One of the most ignorant statements a husband or wife can make is, "I don't want to talk about it!" You may need a good night's sleep—or even a half-hour to think and pray—before discussing a debatable subject, but sweeping a subject under the rug just sets the scene for a later explosion.

A Matter of Life or Death

"Death and life are in the power of the tongue" (Prov. 18:21). Know that you are going to live with the consequences of every word you speak. Your words can add mental and physical health to—or destroy—your marriage and family.

Proverbs 13:3 (LB) says, "Self-control means controlling the tongue! A quick retort can ruin everything." Former First Lady Nancy Reagan said it beautifully: "The difference between a successful marriage and a mediocre one consists in leaving about three or four things a day unsaid!"

Ninety percent of the friction in marriage is caused by one of three things: wrong timing; wrong setting; wrong manner, including wrong volume and/or tone of voice.

If you need to talk through an issue over which you disagree, choose a time when you are both rested and when neither of you is hungry. Most heavy arguments take place when people are too tired to cope or too hungry to be chemically balanced. Choose a quiet and private setting.

Again, speak "the truth in love" (Eph. 4:15). If for the moment you feel you don't love your spouse, let the Lord love your spouse through you. Christ died for that spouse of yours.

A raised voice is always the beginning of an argument; keep your volume level and listenable. But remember, snakes can be venomous even when quiet. "Drop dead," for instance, is a terrible thing to say at any volume.

To end an argument the two most beautiful words you can say are "I'm sorry." To touch your spouse's heart the three most beautiful words you can say are "I love you." To end a debate the four most powerful words you can say are "I guess you're right." To bring healing, wholeness and real joy in your marriage, the one name you can call on is Jesus. Seek Him—the "Wonderful Counselor" (Is. 9:6). Pray together.

Formula for Solving Problems Together

When problems arise that need to be discussed, follow this simple—but powerful—formula.

1. *Define the problem.* Sound familiar? A couple begins to discuss, then one of them gets disgusted. They start arguing. The whole train of thought gets derailed. The fight is on. Instead, begin discussing your problem by defining the point you both want to discuss. Once you are both sure you are on the same wavelength, you'll be ready to discuss the whole issue. Remember, keep the soundness of the best idea more important than making loud sounds.

2. *Discuss ways to solve the problem. Write every possible answer down on paper.* To one trying to make a point quickly and "win," writing things down may seem like a bunch of fuss and bother. But you both need to see what options exist for solving a problem that could otherwise divide you.

Keep in clear focus every one of the possibilities, even the one you may laugh over when it's first suggested. Sometimes you'll discover that that was the best idea of all.

3. *Decide on the best possible option.* Before making the final decision on any important subject, whether it's touchy or not, touch each other and God. Honestly, and with faith, pray together (see James 1:5-8). Sometimes you will both come to a brand new conclusion as you are praying. Sometimes, when one of you has been arguing hotly for his or her own way, God will change that one's mind (see Matt. 7:7-8; Prov. 21:1).

4. *Both of you make a commitment to God and each other to follow that plan.* Husbands, you've been called to "give yourself up" in your marriage (Eph. 5:25). That means dying to selfishness. Wives, you've been called to be "subject" to your husbands "in everything" (Eph. 5:24). That means dying to selfishness. Get God's point? Neither of you has the privilege of being selfish. A self-centered person is off-centered.

Always Verbally Minister Love to Each Other

Job's wife didn't understand this point. At the worst moment of his agony she simply screamed at him, "Curse God and die!" (Job 2:9). With friends like her, who needs enemies?

The Christian life is meant to be spent rejoicing. The apostle Paul wrote the entire book of Philippians while in prison for his Christian witness. It is generally believed that he was chained to two guards twenty-four hours a day. The guards took shifts, but Paul didn't get any shifts. There he was, aching body and aching to get out. Imagine the doom and gloom he could have been writing. Imagine how he could have blamed God. But in the midst of all that he wrote, "Rejoice in the Lord always; again I will say, rejoice!" (Phil 4:4). Paul knew he was in prison for the Lord's glory (see Phil. 1:12-21). That's exactly why you are in your marriage. Paul further wrote, "I have learned to be content in whatever circumstances I am" (Phil. 4:11). For every minute you're mad at someone you lose sixty seconds of happiness.

This doesn't mean Christians will be happy all the time. It means that during tough times we will keep our joyous faith in the God who "causes all things to work together for good to those who love God" (Rom. 8:28).

The Bible warns that staying unhappy or having "organ concerts" (relating what's wrong with every organ in your body) will keep you in constant trouble. "A cheerful heart does good like a medicine, but a broken spirit makes one sick" (Prov. 17:22, LB). "When a man is gloomy, everything seems to go wrong; when he is cheerful, everything seems right!" (Prov. 15:15, LB).

When your spouse is emotionally low, for whatever reason, you, as the husband or wife, are to help lift him or her up again. But how you do this will make all the difference as to whether or not you succeed—or get so frustrated that your spouse's depression depresses you. Don't let the depressed spouse drag you down.

The Right Way and the Wrong Way

Mistakes at this one point can contribute to this sad statistic: Communication breakdown is the number one reason given for divorce.

Ephesians 4:29 gives the right way to help raise a spouse out of depression: "Let no unwholesome word proceed from your mouth, but only such a word as is good for edification [building the person up] according to the need of the moment, that it may give grace to those who hear."

When you verbally attack your depressed spouse you simply depress him or her all the more. Then your spouse will either retreat in an angry silence or blow up, saying things you will both eventually regret. Instead, be kind.

A depressed person needs a friend, a person who walks in when the rest of the world walks out. Be your husband or wife's best friend. No lectures, please. Warm and soothing words will give the mate with a gloomy picture a brand new view of life. You may not be able to change the situation, but you can help change his or her attitude.

Speak encouraging words, but don't say too much. If the slump persists, pray. If he or she will let you, take your spouse's hand and pray out loud. Otherwise pray out of his or her hearing range.

On two different occasions, very late at night, I have been in severe physical pain with no relief in sight. My agony was so great that I could not concentrate on prayer. Both times my darlin' Arlyne laid her hand on me and asked the Lord to release me from the pain. Both times I've immediately gone to sleep and awakened with no pain. Prayer does bring release and relief (see Acts 9:17-19).

There is a wrong way to react to a depressed spouse. Preaching, making jokes or piously quoting Scripture verses—meant to strengthen the depressed spouse or lead him or her out of the problem—almost never bring healing; these actions often churn up anger. As for making light of the situation, Proverbs 25:20 (LB) explains, "Being happy-go-lucky around a person whose heart is heavy is as bad as stealing his jacket in cold weather, or rubbing salt in his wounds."

As for glibly quoting Scripture, even if the depressed person understands your intent and the intent of the verse, your actions can prompt feelings of condemnation that aggravate the depression. Your spouse's faith level is probably near zero at this point, and the devil will take advantage of the situation. He's "the accuser of our brethren" (Rev. 12:10). As one man told me, "I don't need a devil. My wife does all the accusing for him."

To be powerful, Scripture has to be received in the human spirit. At a time when God seems to have gone on vacation, it seldom helps to hear someone say, "Well, if you'd just trust God it would all be different, (and here's a verse to prove my point)." It isn't that you are wrong about that verse. It is that your glib quoting of a verse may make this person feel as if you are "rubbing salt" into his or her wounds. Again, pray—out loud if possible, privately if not.

Never pick at your spouse. It is sin to make someone mad on purpose (see Matt. 5:43-48). One of the most foolish lies that came out of childhood was "Sticks and stones may break my bones, but words will never hurt me." Words can hurt! Each of you knows that saying certain things to your spouse would be like waving a red cape at a bull. Don't say these things. Tell the Lord instead.

"Rejoice with those who rejoice, and weep with those who weep" (Rom. 12:15) asks that you identify where someone is emotionally and minister to that level of emotion. "Rejoice with those who rejoice." That includes at home, even daily. Do you act as though you were baptized in sour pickle juice? "Weep with those who weep" doesn't mean you're to join in with the moody blues. Rather, minister to anyone who has those blues and work with the Lord to set that person free.

Remember, a Christ-centered pastor or counselor often can help one work through blues that hang on. So can a godly doctor, if the problem is physical. Recommend it, but don't push. Let God bring the healing however He's going to do it as you pray. Prayer does change things.

Learn to Listen

Why do you suppose women like strong, silent men? They think such men are listening!

One of the greatest honors of my life was interviewing Billy Graham on radio. What impressed me most was how he riveted his attention on me. His eyes pierced me. Though I interviewed him in a crowded room, he listened intently to my every word. He answered every question with great skill and total humility. As we spoke, I was amazed to learn that he had spent most of the night on a plane, on which he had been unable to sleep. Is it any wonder that Billy Graham is considered one of the greatest men of our day? What a communicator—and what a listener! Those two traits go together like hand and glove. Wives long for husbands who listen like Billy Graham.

I often hear a complaint from husbands: Their wives drive them up the wall by saying something "a thousand times." As one husband put it, "My wife has never gotten the point that Jesus said to avoid vain repetition!" (see Matt. 6:7). But a husband can end that problem easily—by listening. Put the newspaper down. Turn off the television set. Listen to each other. In fact, every night you men need to sit your wives down and give them a good listening to!

An Australian wife described the situation in so many homes. "It's not what he does; it's what he doesn't do. He's a marvelous provider. He gets up at six and is out of the house by seven, and I don't see him again until eight at night. He's a plumber with his own company. I do his bookkeeping. We have two children and everything material in the world. But when he comes in, I can tell you what he will do, every single day: He'll open the door, kiss me on the cheek, ask me if my day was OK, take a cup of tea, sit in the chair and tune out for the rest of the evening. The kids could start a world war, and he wouldn't notice. He'll probably put the television on and sleep through the programs. Come bedtime, he'll try a kiss and a cuddle, and if I seem in the mood, he can make fantastic love. We've always been good together that way. But if I don't respond at once, he'll flop back on his side and snore. And these days I'm so angry I'm never in the mood. I've told him things have got to change, but he just stands there looking silly and saying, 'What on earth do you want me to do?' How do I tell him I just want him to *be there?*"

Act Like a Mirror

Think of a mirror—reflecting whatever is in its way. In many ways communication is just that simple: In a meaningful conversation, each should understand the other's point of view then be able to prove that he or she understands the other's point of view.

Bill Gaultiere says, "It's amazing how many spouses don't seem to know their mates have any real feelings. A wife will be sitting in my office pouring her heart out to her husband. He'll just be sitting there, staring. Maybe he'll nod. If he says anything at all, he mutters simplistic and meaningless words: 'I understand exactly how you feel.'

"Or he'll begin sharing his feelings, and then she'll jump in and defend herself, trying so hard to protect herself that she's not listening to his feelings—just his comments about her. As a counselor I see that the hurting spouse really wants to be heard and sense someone cares about what's happening to him or her."

When Bill finds either the husband or wife has been deaf to the spouse, he often teaches the two how to play "the mirror game." Bill tells the couple, "It's important that you give your spouse feedback, repeating back what you think you've heard. Say, 'Honey, what I think you're saying is....' This way your spouse will know whether or not you really heard what he [or she] meant to say. If you didn't understand correctly, play the game again until you agree that you've got it."

Unless your rage level has come to a place where you are angry with each other every time you try to communicate, try this mirror game. (If it *has* come to that point, see a counselor or get to a Marriage Plus seminar—fast.)

The Thirty-Minute Challenge

If I asked you, "Is daily prayer important?" or, "Is daily Bible study important?" you'd probably answer yes. And what is prayer and Bible study? A time of focusing your attention on God.

Is your marriage important? Are you spending daily time with your wife—time when just the two of you alone concentrate your love on each other? A husband and wife need to spend at least thirty minutes a day alone in communication. I'm not talking about a half-hour for sex. (That may require a second hour.)

If you've let your kids know you love them, they will eventually be glad that you set aside a certain time each day to communicate alone with your spouse. They will surely benefit from your private time. When the children are very young you can take your private time after they're in bed. Later, just let them know that they are always to be in another room (out of earshot) during that time.

Schedule this special half-hour when you are both as wide awake as possible. If you *both* enjoy mornings, you may want to set aside a half-hour before the kids are up. Night owls may prefer a midnight rendezvous, as long as it doesn't make either of you cranky in the morning.

This half-hour, set aside for verbal love, should never be for criticizing or arguing. If one of you turns this into a gripe session, the other will likely want to cancel the tradition. Use part of this time for prayer and perhaps to share a Scripture verse with each other. Spend the rest of the time in loving communication—for the sake of being with each other.

No television watching, which creates silence. But enjoy thirty minutes of fellowship and positive, constructive communication, which can become the most important half-hour of your day.

Pray Together

The strongest power in the universe will never be a bomb. It won't be any invention made by man. Far more powerful than any destructive force, satanic or otherwise, is prayer.

"Again I say to you, that if two of you agree on earth about anything that they may ask, it shall be done for them by My Father who is in heaven" (Matt. 18:19-20).

Agreeing prayer is the single greatest human power in the universe. God has called husbands and wives to come together and agree.

Let me give you three quick tips about praying together:

1. *Don't necessarily pray just before bedtime.* If you find praying just before bedtime a real blessing, by all means pray then. But for the rest of us—why are we going to bed? Usually because we are tired, and it's rude to fall asleep on someone, especially on God! I frequently hear this complaint from Christian husbands or wives who don't want to pray with their spouses: "We kneel down by the side of our bed when I'm already exhausted. Then he (or she) wants to go on and on and on. If I fall asleep, I'm suddenly jabbed in the ribs and called 'unspiritual.' "

So when should a couple pray together? When you are both wide awake. Right after dinner often works well, but it depends on your daily schedules.

2. *Don't preach—pray!* Even more often I hear this complaint from Christian husbands or wives who don't want to pray with their spouses: "When my spouse starts praying, he (or she) attacks me! 'O Lord, cause

my husband to....' Or, 'O Lord, forgive my wife for....' '' That's preaching, not praying, and it isn't allowed. It will ruin any "agreeing" in prayer.

3. *Keep it short!* The number-one complaint I hear from Christian wives or husbands who refuse to pray with their spouses is: "The prayers take too long. I just get bored listening. I lose all sense of the presence of God. My mind starts wandering, and I get to feeling sacrilegious."

God never tires of hearing us pray, but your husband or wife might. Yet, if you both take heartfelt praise and needs to God together and thank Him for answered prayer, you can usually cover high priorities in five to ten minutes. Of course, as you discover the amazing power of agreeing prayer, it won't be surprising if you both find a desire to pray longer.

You'll also want to have private, individual, daily prayer sessions. There you can talk to God at greater length. If you are too busy to pray, you are too busy. You haven't got a prayer without prayer.

The finest book on prayer I've ever read is *Prayer Is Invading the Impossible* (Ballantine/Epiphany Books), written by my own pastor, Jack Hayford. If prayer seems difficult to you at all, please read that book.

Unless you are spending more time doing these things already, fifteen minutes in prayer and fifteen minutes in individual or united Bible study every day will continually strengthen your walk with God. You can find that much time by giving up one television program. Go for it!

> To sum up, let all be harmonious, sympathetic, brotherly, kind-hearted, and humble in spirit; not returning evil for evil, or insult for insult, but giving a blessing instead; for you were called for the very purpose that you might inherit a blessing.
> For,
> "Let him who means to love life and see good days
> Refrain his [or her] tongue from evil and his lips from
> speaking guile.
> And let him turn away from evil and do good;
> Let him seek peace and pursue it.
> For the eyes of the Lord are upon the righteous,
> And His ears attend to their prayer,
> But the face of the Lord is against those who do evil."
> 1 Peter 3:8-12

WHAT MAKES EATING YOUR WORDS SO DIFFICULT IS SWALLOWING YOUR PRIDE AT THE SAME TIME!

Questions for Reflection and Discussion

1. Husbands, after reading this chapter and the chapters for husbands, can you think of anything you are doing—or not doing—that may make your wife feel as if she cannot communicate her feelings with you? What will happen if her feelings build up inside and she feels she has no outlet? What can you do to help her *want* to share her feelings with you? Memorize Hebrews 4:14-16 and Ephesians 4:15.

2. How are prayer and communication with your spouse alike? What things most hinder your ability to communicate with God? What things most hinder your communication with your spouse? What similarities do you see?

3. Does the most effective communication between you and your spouse take place on the spur of the moment (wherever and whenever), or do you plan times when you sit and talk without interruption? Make an agreement that from now on you will spend one half-hour alone with each other every day or night to communicate. In your first scheduled half-hour together, read the preceding chapter out loud and discuss it. (This may require several sessions.) If you have any major area of disagreement, follow the formula given for solving problems together. Whether or not you are having problems, follow the rules about praying together. Memorize Philippians 2:1-4 and Ephesians 4:29.

4. The apostle Paul wrote the entire book of Philippians while in prison. Sometimes people tell me their marriage seems "like a prison." Read the book of Philippians. List at least six times Paul praises God in the midst of situations most people would consider unfair or horrible. List at least three of Paul's keys to happiness. Memorize James 5:13 and 1 Thessalonians 5:16-18.

5. Note Proverbs 25:20 in the *Living Bible*: "Being happy-go-lucky around a person whose heart is heavy is as bad as stealing his jacket in cold weather, or rubbing salt in his wounds." What is your usual response when your spouse is depressed? What should it be? Study Romans 12:15

in the context of Ephesians 2:9-21. Write a paragraph that describes the essence of Romans 12:15. Read Ephesians 4:29 and write a paragraph that describes the essence of that verse. Memorize Proverbs 25:20 (LB); Romans 12:15; and Ephesians 4:29.

6. The Bible says very little about listening and a great deal about hearing. What does it mean to be an "active listener"? Paraphrase on paper Proverbs 12:15 and James 1:19-20. Memorize these verses.

Dear Ray,

My wife and I have been married fifty-five years. We were childhood sweethearts, and that's never stopped. We've always been in love with each other and with the Lord. So how did you help us, Ray? Far more than you could ever realize. You taught us about sex!

You'd think a couple married fifty-five years would know all about sex, especially since we've had three kids. But I want you to know—and you can share this too—my wife and I have gone through a horrible amount of needless guilt because no one, until you, had ever told us what God says about sex. All we'd ever heard before was legalistic and rigid. We never heard God wanted sex in marriage to be fun. When we had "fun" in our sex life, we felt guilty. The conscience is a horrible thing when you don't know what the Bible says about something, because it can condemn you when God doesn't. Until you, I'd never heard anyone so blunt and biblical at the same time.

Thank God, even after fifty-five years, He sent you to us. May He send you to every married couple hurting with needless guilt. Thanks for Marriage Plus.

Never Too Old to Learn

*"The wife does not
have authority over her own
body, but the husband does; and
likewise also the husband does
not have authority over his own
body, but the wife does."*

1 Corinthians 7:4

TWELVE

Pure Sex

**SEX IS THE MOST FUN ANY MARRIED COUPLE
CAN HAVE WITHOUT SMILING!**

The session on "Sex in Marriage" during the Marriage Plus seminar lasts
for more than two hours. It is a very popular session, filled with a lot
of laughs and much more than I can share with you here. Your attitude
toward the subject of sex in marriage has most likely been shaped by
somebody's opinion—or just your own opinion—unless, of course, you
have already seen what the Bible has to say. You can find everything from
the most liberal view (*"Anything* goes!") to the most narrow view ("If
you *must* do it, be in bed, fully clothed, with the blankets up and the lights
out—thinking about vegetables all the while.")

God's Plan

God has designed a great plan to keep sexual sin from happening: it's
called marriage (1 Cor. 7:2). The plan began in a garden of paradise before
any sin ever darkened our planet. Until the serpent came to spoil things,
the only thing that wasn't good in that garden was man's aloneness (see
Gen. 2:18). Even before sin entered the human picture, God brought naked
Eve to Adam (Gen. 2:21-22), and as husband and wife they probably fully
enjoyed sexual love.

And the Lord God said, "It isn't good for man to be alone; I will

make a companion for him, a helper suited to his needs.''
"...This is it!'' Adam exclaimed. "She is part of my own bone and flesh! Her name is 'woman' because she was taken out of a man.'' This explains why a man leaves his father and mother and is joined to his wife in such a way that the two become one person. Now although the man and his wife were both naked, neither of them was embarrassed or ashamed (Gen. 2:18, 23-25, LB).

One of the happiest moments of any marriage is when a husband and his wife can stand naked before each other and be unashamed. Many imagine Adam was extremely handsome and Eve stunningly beautiful. But the Bible doesn't say this. One thing for sure, in the garden they were not comparing themselves with other humans. They only had eyes for each other. That is what love—and God—requires.

Satan Perverted Sex

In John 10:10 Jesus Christ told us He came to bring abundant life; He then told us "the thief" (identified as the devil) breaks in to steal, destroy and kill that abundant life. The devil's obviously able to do this in the sexual arena of marriage. But remember: As Christians we have been given authority over the devil (see James 4:7-8; 1 Cor. 7:5); when we use that authority we will realize great sex in marriage is spiritual warfare.

Recently, in Australia, the wife of a Christian leader said, "I want to thank you for what you said about sex in marriage. God's Word through you has set me free." Then she explained she had been married sixteen years and, "Quite frankly, sex has been a nightmare to me. I was raped before I was married. My husband never knew. I didn't enjoy sex, and he thought it was his fault. Well, last night was the most thrilling—and fulfilling—night my husband and I have ever known. I was able to give myself to him freely. And I'm eager for sex with him now. Yes, I've been set free, and my husband is free too." I rejoiced with her, though I was reminded of how all too common her problem is.

According to nationwide research done by the Domestic Violence Project, one in three American women and one in five men were sexually abused as children or teenagers.[1] Rape has increased 400 percent in the past thirty years. Many otherwise wonderful husbands and wives fear sex even with their own spouses, or are disgusted by it, because of frightening sexual incidents or feelings of guilt in their own backgrounds.

God Invented Sex

But before Satan perverted sex, God invented it. In 1970 Larry Christenson started the whole wave of Christian books on marriage with his best-seller *The Christian Family* (Bethany Fellowship). I enjoyed his whole book, but my favorite line asks, "Isn't there anybody around to say that sex is fun?"

Well, I say it. In fact, I urge married couples to say it to each other. (If no one but your spouse is within earshot, put down this book for a minute and shout happily to your spouse, "Sex is fun!")

Many emotionally hurting people claim that sex is an "animal thing." But humans and animals differ greatly in their very reason for sex. Animals mate only when it is possible to impregnate, and pleasure is simply a by-product of the act. Yet God has made pleasure a chief ingredient in the husband-wife relationship.

Had God intended sex only as a way to produce babies, He would have removed the ability for women to have sex once they reached menopause. But sex isn't meant to achieve anything. It's not done to prove a man is a man or a woman is a woman. God intends sex between a husband and his wife to be deeply fulfilling, a passionate intimacy making two different people "one" for a lifetime.

From the beginning of recorded history the male libido has been the subject of everything from poetry to bad jokes. But for many centuries large segments of society have argued that women have no natural sex drive. In England during Queen Victoria's day homosexuality was outlawed but lesbianism wasn't. It was understood that some men might express their sex drive in such a savage manner, but no woman would possibly do such a thing!

The truth is God put a wonderful sex drive in woman. In fact, it can be said that women are much more sexual than men. A woman can have multiple climaxes; few men can. If a man does have multiple climaxes, the first is always the most intense. A woman's successive climaxes can be increasingly ecstatic. The clitoris ("little key" in Latin, as it is the "key" to unlocking her sexual response) is the only part of the human body made for one purpose only: pleasure.

God is delighted when His people have great sex lives in their marriages. Look at this passage:

> "My beloved extended his hand through the opening,
> And my feelings were aroused for him. I arose to open to my
>   beloved;
> And my hands dripped with myrrh,
> And my fingers with liquid myrrh,
> On the handles of the bolt" (Song 5:4-5).

The Song of Solomon, though it makes many vital comments to the church, is basically the story of a husband and wife and their lovemaking.

The finest discussion on this is Joseph C. Dillow's classic *Solomon on Sex* (Thomas Nelson). His point and ours is that God has always intended the sex act to be far more than just an act. It is not gland calling out to gland, but a husband expressing total devotion to a wife who has given her life into his hands and trusts him fully with her body and her heart. This commitment can be known only by those who dare to work together for a lifetime.

It comes as a surprise to many people that God has any rules about sex in marriage. It comes as a surprise to many others that God doesn't outlaw sex entirely. But in the many years I've been studying the Bible I have discovered God does have four rules about sex. Like the law of gravity, these laws are made by God to hold things together, namely a marriage. Any violation of these four rules will greatly limit God's ability to bless a marriage and will bring great threat to a lasting relationship.

1. Sex is exclusively designed for a husband and wife, completely alone with each other (see Gen. 2:24-25).

2. No sexual act should be entered into if it offends either spouse (see Eph. 5:22-25).

3. No pain must be involved in the sex act (see Gen. 6:13).

4. Sex must be an act of giving and not of forcing (see Phil. 2:3-4).

In 1 Corinthians 7:1-5 God gives His fullest instructions for sex in marriage. Here's the whole passage, which we will break down and study one thought at a time:

> Now concerning the things about which you wrote, it is good for

a man not to touch a woman. But because of immoralities, let each man have his own wife, and let each woman have her own husband. Let the husband fulfill his duty to his wife, and likewise also the wife to her husband. The wife does not have authority over her own body, but the husband does; and likewise also the husband does not have authority over his own body, but the wife does. Stop depriving one another, except by agreement for a time that you may devote yourselves to prayer, and come together again lest Satan tempt you because of your lack of self-control.

One Spouse

Here again are verses 1-2: 'Now concerning the things about which you wrote, it is good for a man not to touch a woman. But because of immoralities, let each man have his own wife, and let each woman have her own husband.''

The apostle Paul wrote to Christians facing the terrible years when many would be martyred for their faith—burned at the stake or fed to lions. At such a horrible moment in history, he said it would probably be better for a man not to "touch a woman." We can hardly imagine the emotional trauma of the husbands or wives who lost their spouses to the satanic horrors of Paul's day. Yet even at such a dreadful time (see 1 Cor. 7:26-28), Paul said it was better to marry than to kill the human sex drive. God never changes (see Mal. 3:6), and His statement "It is not good for the man to be alone; I will make a helper suitable for him" (Gen. 2:18) should be considered a fact for all time.

In this passage Paul again forbids sex outside of marriage. Let me paraphrase: "But because many would be immoral if they did not marry, let each man have his own wife, and let each woman have her own husband." In God's judgment, sex without marriage is immoral and forbidden (see Heb. 13:4; 1 Cor. 6:18).

Today many churchgoers are so unaware of God's Word that they feel they have God's blessings on their living together without legal marriage. Like the adulteress in Proverbs 7:14, they say, "I've paid my vows" to God; they believe God endorses their sin and has actually brought the two of them together. But once a Christian knows God's Word, he or she *will* obey God. As Jesus Christ said, "If you love Me, you will keep My commandments'' (John 14:15). ''But I say, walk by the Spirit, and you will not carry out the desire of the flesh'' (Gal. 5:16).

First Timothy 3:2, 12 tells elders and deacons that they must be ''the husband of one wife.'' This is the biblical pattern from the beginning of time (see Gen. 2:24) and the only New Testament pattern.

The meaning of the original Greek word translated ''the husband of one wife'' according to many outstanding Bible scholars, including G. Campbell Morgan, is ''a one-woman man.'' An ornery pit bulldog is usually called ''a one-man dog,'' meaning that a bulldog will be totally loyal to its owner for as long as it lives. But it loves just *one* person. Nobody else! In the same way, in the sexual sense, a man who is a church leader must be a ''one-woman man,'' and a woman must be a ''one-man woman.''

Many Christians have fallen into adultery because they were not ''one-woman men'' or ''one-man women.'' Whether married or single, the cry from God's heart is, ''Flee immorality!'' because of the tragic results this sin always brings to individual lives, to their nation (see 1 Cor. 6:18-20) and ultimately to the immoral person himself or herself (see Rev. 21:8).

Hebrews 13:4 stresses that marriage makes sex a pure experience between a husband and wife. It tell us, ''Let marriage be held in honor among all, and let the marriage bed be undefiled; for fornicators and adulterers God will judge.''

The Greek word translated *undefiled* in Hebrews 13:4 means ''without blemish, complete, full, perfect, sincerely sound, without spot, upright; that which is not dirty, foul, corrupt or unclean.''

In *The Act of Marriage* (Bantam Books) Tim and Beverly LaHaye have written, ''Nothing could be clearer than the statement [in Hebrews 13:4] that 'the marriage bed is undefiled.' Anyone who suggests anything amiss between husband and wife in regard to the act of marriage simply does *not* understand the Scriptures.''

The ''marriage bed'' is designed exclusively for a husband and wife, completely alone in loving privacy (see Gen. 2:24-25). Most women can't fully relax to enjoy sex unless they are completely alone with their husbands. Children, even babies, should be somewhere else during times of foreplay and intercourse. Even small children can find such parental behavior frightening, confusing or even intriguing. Singles of any age should be kept far removed from the sight or sounds of sex until it is their joy to enter into marriage.

As for others who aren't single, feeding sexual fantasy by anyone other than your spouse is specifically condemned by God (see Matt. 5:28-29). He condemns both exhibitionism and voyeurism (see 1 John 2:15-17). As Job said in Job 31:1 (Amplified), "I dictated a covenant—an agreement—to my eyes; how then could I look (lustfully) upon a girl?" In a day when the mass media are constantly pushing lust and sleaze, every Christian needs to dictate a moral covenant with his or her eyes.

Sex was never intended to be casual. It is a priceless present never to be unwrapped until marriage. Opened early, this gift never satisfies.

The Sexual Assignment

First Corinthians 7:3: "Let the husband fulfill his duty to his wife, and likewise also the wife to her husband."

Considering themselves worldly wise, some people have laughed at the apostle Paul's word choice, calling sexual intercourse in marriage a duty. Yet the meaning of the Greek word for "duty" is "a required assignment." God requires sex as part—a frequent part—of marriage. Many who travel, as I do, know how important such an assignment is whenever we are with our spouses. Those who are together daily are more apt to enjoy sex only as something to be done once in a while or when they have the time. Enthusiasm is contagious, and so is the lack of it. Paul says sex is a "duty" for a husband and wife to perform regularly; it's never to be placed on the back burner of a marriage. If your spouse wants sexual fulfillment, Paul says, "Give it!" even if you are tired, don't feel much like doing it or would rather play Monopoly.

Plain ordinary tiredness is probably the most common single problem working against a successful sexual relationship. That's why sexual play and intercourse are often far better at some time other than bedtime, when one or both of you are just "too tired." Your water bed should never become the Dead Sea.

Once in a while an "energy crisis" that renders a spouse unable to have sex should be forgiven instantly. But in marriage, prolonged lapses of sexual foreplay and intercourse are unnatural and in need of the Lord's ministry through a wise, godly counselor or doctor who understand's God's joyful word on sex in marriage.

211

Sexual Authority

First Corinthians 7:4: "The wife does not have authority over her own body, but the husband does; and likewise also the husband does not have authority over his own body, but the wife does."

The Greek word translated as *authority* means "the right of, the jurisdiction over, the power of." The Bible tells a wife she is to relinquish the sexual rights of her body to her husband. Likewise, the husband is to relinquish the sexual rights of his body to his wife. From the wedding on, the body of each spouse is given to the other.

Aside from God's four biblical rules about sex stated earlier in this chapter, anyone claiming to have the right to take the sexual authority away from the husband and his wife and legislate new "rights" and "wrongs" for them—as long as the married couple both enjoy what they are doing—is greatly violating God's Word. It's amazing how many people will defend the Bible in every other passage of Scripture except those defining who has the authority when it comes to married sex.

Revelation 22:18-19 warns that it is as sinful to *add* to what the Bible says as it is to *subtract* from it. A counselor who does either one is dangerously out of order. The word *lasciviousness* (see Gal. 5:19-21; Eph. 4:17-24; Jude 4, KJV) means "the act of creating moral rules that disagree with God's moral rules." Feelings about what God would say don't count. God's Word does (see John 14:23-24).

Serve One Another

A word to husbands or wives who would take ungodly advantage of 1 Corinthians 7:3-4: An emotionally scarred wife cried to me, "All my husband wants from me is sex. I can't remember the last time he sat down, looked me in the eyes and told me he loved me. We haven't had a meaningful conversation in years. All he wants is my body!"

Her husband interjected, "But the Bible says that when I want sex, she's got to give it to me. It says it's her duty." That man was as cold as a corpse. He was treating his wife like a meat market and treating God's Word like a stack of sweaters in a department store bargain basement—picking and choosing what he wanted and discarding the rest. I handed him the Bible and asked him to read Ephesians 5:25, "Husbands, love your wives, just as Christ also loved the church and gave Himself up for her.'' Then I had him read Galatians 5:13 (KJV), ''Use not liberty for an occasion to the flesh, but by love serve one another.'' He looked at me sheepishly and said, ''Oh, yeah. I hadn't thought about *that*.''

Antonio in William Shakespeare's *The Merchant of Venice* said, ''The devil can cite Scripture for his purpose!'' Antonio was right. First Corinthians 7:4 calls for mutual submission in the area of sex. Both the husband and the wife are to enjoy the sex act.

The husband who demands, ''You have to submit to me!'' but then ignores the rest of the Bible is a hypocrite. In sex, she does *not* have to submit to him. She needs to love him, and he needs to love her. First Corinthians 7:4 is very clear: Both married partners must agree on what they enjoy or don't enjoy in sex and do only what they enjoy together. Acts of sex that make one or the other spouse feel degraded are not acts of love.

Some husbands make the terrible mistake of equating romance with sex. They treat their wives as a three-step assembly line: (1) kiss her; (2) touch her breasts; (3) have intercourse. Wives who are rushed or forced into sex without adequate loving intimacy feel used and violated—because they *have* been used and violated.

Forcing a spouse into any unwelcome sexual act will damage your spouse's ability to trust any further sexual relationship. God-blessed passion and rape are exact opposites.

Selfishness—what Philippians 2:3 calls an ''empty conceit''—is the exact opposite of agape love. It is ''empty'' because it will prove to be worthless and accomplish nothing but harm. This is especially true in marriage.

Give love and you will receive it (see Luke 6:38). Guys, the excuse that you're just not romantic means that you're just not thoughtful. Don't be too selfish and preoccupied with your own life and your own problems to take the time and make the effort to act romantically toward your wife.

Forced sexual acts are wrong; what's more, no sexual act should be entered into if it offends either spouse (see Eph. 5:22-25). Whatever threatens to weaken the enthusiasm and vitality of a marriage is a harmful substitute for love. Shaming a mate by doing what he or she considers lewd or obscene will only damage the marriage relationship and make sex far less enjoyable than God has intended it to be.

On the other hand, a *prude* has been defined as someone who whispers sweet nothing-doings in your ear. If you were raised in a one-parent home or had parents who seldom or never touched, you may never have learned the vital need for touch or sex in marriage.

The *agape*-love attitude for both partners should be, "I want to please you, honey. I want to give you all the love I can. And I want you to passionately enjoy my body because it belongs to you."

If your attitude is not based on love for your spouse, please seek knowledgeable Christian counsel to help you find a healthier look at life and marriage.

A further word about what sexual relations should not involve. Genesis 6:13 indicates that pain is not God's intention for the natural sex act. Except for the breaking of the hymen on the wedding night, pain is almost always a physical cry that something unnatural and wrong is happening. (Today many women break their hymens before having intercourse, through rigorous exercise in gym classes, etc.) If any recurring pain takes place during lovemaking, a competent doctor should be consulted immediately.

Sadism and sado-masochism are ruled out by God, as they bring great harm to the body and the mind. Whips, chains or any other instruments of torture are never expressions of love.

Anal sex is also ruled out by God because of its high risk of infection and disease. If often kills.

Affection and infection never go together. Avoid kissing any part of your spouse's body if cold sores or any other known infection could be transferred. If an infection is ongoing, consult a godly doctor for advice regarding safeguards.

Although "cleanliness is next to godliness" isn't a biblical saying, it is a true saying when it comes to sex in marriage. Daily baths or showers, clean teeth and breath, clean and trimmed fingernails, clean hair, underarm deodorant, etc., are all essential "sex aids." One thing nice about being a man is you don't have to kiss someone with a three-day-old beard. (Guys, shave or trim that beard daily.)

Leviticus 15:19-24 says a husband is ceremonially unclean if he has intercourse with his wife during her menstruation. Of course, we live under the New Covenant and do not have to be concerned with the ceremonial laws. But some wives do have pain during menstruation (and sometimes just before), and a husband should be careful not to cause her more discomfort. Also, some doctors warn of a greater possibility of infection for a woman during her menstrual flow. But some wives find their sex drive heightened during their menstruation. Even at this time of month be willing to fulfill a spouse's sexual needs.

In his excellent cassette and study album "Sex Problems and Sex Techniques in Marriage," Ed Wheat, another outstanding authority on the Bible and sex, says: "There is no wrongness in married sex as long as the husband or wife do not offend each other or give a sense of discomfort to each other."

When each spouse exercises love—and never force—in sex, the other spouse's passion will grow immeasurably, wanting to please and meet the desires of the loving partner.

As Keith Intrater says in his informative book *Covenant Relationships,* "The dynamics of sexuality are more spiritual and psychological than they are physical. If a husband will minister security to his wife, she will be able to relax. Everything about your marriage, including your sexual relationship, will improve. If a woman will yield to her husband's authority, he will feel more confident and there will be greater harmony in the home. The sexual relationship is the privilege of intimacy that is earned by commitment to the marriage covenant."[2]

Make Love, Not War!

First Corinthians 7:5: "Stop depriving one another, except by agreement for a time that you may devote yourselves to prayer, and come together again lest Satan tempt you because of your lack of self-control."

This verse makes four vital points about sex in marriage:

1. *"Stop depriving one another...."* Keep on telling each other what you enjoy. God makes man and woman "normal" by creating the greatest ecstasy in the freest and most secure of settings—in marriage. Marriage is for lovemaking.

The Greek word translated *deprive* means "to sexually stimulate but not righteously satisfy." (That is why a single person can't "righteously" pet on a date. It involves sexually stimulating someone while righteous satisfaction is impossible.) Once a couple is married, whenever either partner is sexually stimulated, the spouse is to "righteously satisfy" the sexual urge.

Paul is saying there is to be no holding back from sex in marriage. Married sex is not a favor; it isn't to be treated as a reward. It isn't like licorice: If you don't like it, you don't have to have it! In marriage you have to have it.

In New Zealand I heard David Edwards, president emeritus of Elim Bible Institute in Lima, New York, and author of the excellent book *The Joy of Intimacy*, speak on the subject of sexual foreplay in marriage: "It's a pity we even call it 'foreplay.' Because when we call it 'fore,' what we are underlining is that it is only the preliminary and that the real delight comes afterwards. That's not necessarily so. It is perfectly proper for the husband and wife to indulge in caressing which might be very intimate and sexual without necessarily taking that caressing to the climax of orgasm and ejaculation." He added that, though he wished we could use some word other than *foreplay,* "I'm quite happy with the word *play.*"

Get to know each other's bodies. Some people like their ears nibbled, their necks caressed, their hair played with, their feet rubbed. Ask your spouse what he or she would like you to do. Express what you would like. While you are touching, ask, "Does this feel good?" Some things married couples say in the midst of passion would shock any other ear or be out of place at any other time. But during foreplay, intercourse or afterglow such words are blessed by God. (Read the Song of Solomon and take note of the things Solomon and the Shulammite said to each other. They may shock you!)

Work at finding creative ways to show your wife you love her. Be affectionate with her without demands for sex. Initiate loving communication with her. The most important sex organ in the human body is the brain. Most women want tender, loving communication from their husbands before sex. In fact, communicate love to her all the time—she's going to be turned off if you speak tenderly only when you want sex.

Touch and kiss sensitive parts of her body, stimulating her before intercourse.

In her book *Forever My Love* (Harvest House), Margaret Hardisty wrote some of the greatest words of sexual counsel for all husbands:

> Whatever you do, don't rush her. A man who thinks five minutes
> is enough preparation is kidding himself. That length of time is
> welcome only to the woman who isn't enjoying her experience

and wants to get it over with. Be prepared to take whatever time is necessary. Let her decide and you react accordingly. Generally twenty minutes to a half hour is realistic, if she is in the habit of reaching a climax. But forty-five minutes to an hour may be necessary as you start to discover each other all over again. Sometimes women like to be handled passionately, and sometimes gently. You'll have to heed your understanding and her response concerning that. But, usually a good rule is to keep your caresses gentle until her passions begin to rise. Her intimate parts shouldn't be approached right away either. The body is a beautiful thing to behold and to caress. If your wife has a block about you touching any part of her body, or her touching any part of your body, she needs to be released from her unnatural fears, for her reluctance is no virtue. Indeed, certain parts of her body have to be caressed at length, with her willing participation, if she's ever to enjoy sexual arousal and the final delight of orgasm....A husband needs to become skillful in manipulating and gently massaging her clitoris, patiently and at length, before actual intercourse. A woman's breasts are also a point of contact for sexual arousement, especially the nipples. But, remember, a wife's breasts or her clitoris shouldn't be pressed hard unless she indicates to you that's what she wants. If the husband will continue to massage the clitoris and the nipples, and continues caressing his wife in sensitive places, he'll bring her to the point of signaling when she's ready for intercourse.

While this is true, a husband often wants to feel like a "he-man" lover whose wife can't get enough of his passion. Ladies, let your husbands believe they're irresistible. A husband needs visual and physical stimulation as he prepares for intercourse, so touch him and also show him what he likes to see. Leave off the hair curlers. Dress (or undress) to please him. And leave at least a dim light on. You want him making love to *you*, not lying in the dark trying to remember what you look like.

A few years ago a gifted woman, Marabel Morgan, wrote a book that shocked many people, though then it quickly became a nationwide Christian best-seller—*The Total Woman* (Fleming Revell). One of many suggestions Marabel made to wives probably caught the most publicity: making and then wearing "peek-a-boo nightgowns" to greet their men at the door as they came home from work. Marabel's plan worked for many wives whose husbands were startled and then ecstatic. But one wife told me that Marabel's plan had backfired for her. Seeing her in a nightgown, her husband accused her of sleeping all day.

No real lover wants to turn his or her lover off. Wife, don't try to hold back your passion. But, husbands, you may have to hold back to avoid premature ejaculation, which is one of the most frustrating problems to both husband and wife. In their book *The Gift of Sex* (Word Books) Clifford and Joyce Penner say the man with this problem is usually "overly goal-oriented," subconsciously feeling that the faster he achieves orgasm the "more masculine" he is. Premature ejaculation can rob a couple of full sexual satisfaction, which can create destructive male guilt. Playing no blame-game, a husband and wife should cooperate—slow and easy. The Penners' book has in-depth answers to this common problem.

After both of you have climaxed, linger with each other. In this romantic afterglow time, simply hold each other, thanking your spouse for being such a great lover. You were made for each other. Hallelujah!

2. *"Stop depriving one another, except by agreement for a time that you may devote yourselves to prayer"* (1 Cor. 7:5).

Although Paul is emphasizing the extreme need for a married couple to fulfill the spouse's sexual needs, here is an exception. This verse clearly underlines the vital need for prayer. Sometimes the need is so urgent that everything else should be stopped to give full attention to God. Days may be spent in earnest, solitary prayer. The King James Bible added the words "and fasting," since many Christians fast during this kind of intense prayer. But note that a married person is to enter into this kind of prayer only "by agreement for a time."

If you feel called to a time of praying like this, what should you do? Well, you mustn't just start praying. Your spouse must agree. Suppose, however, that your spouse said, "No. I don't want you to fast, because when you fast you're grumpy." Ironically, they would be agreeing with God, as Isaiah 58:3-6 makes it clear that God isn't pleased with grumpy fasts.

Since we are just supposing, suppose your husband or wife said, "No. I want sex with you, and you are never interested in sex when you are fasting." In 1 Corinthians 7:5 God says that if you were to rank the importance of fasting or sex or the extended time of prayer that would break the regular enjoyment of marital sex, sex is the most important. The two of you must agree on the temporary abstinence or there should be none.

3. "...*and come together again...*" (1 Cor. 7:5). Talk about being blunt! Only people ignorant of his writings call the apostle Paul a prude. Long seasons of prayer, especially when accompanied by fasting, can sap energy and dissipate the sex drive. Here Paul is saying, "If you do let sex go so you can fast or pray and then begin to gain back any energy, you're quickly to have sexual intercourse with your spouse."

Someone has said, "Sex is something that evolves over the years from tri-weekly to try weekly to try weakly!" May it never be so in your marriage.

In each marriage the person who seems to have the lesser sexual desire needs to be very considerate of the needs of the other. Once a month might seem fine to one spouse, while every other day appeals to the other. God says, "Do it!" (Martin Luther did say, "Twice a week." So the matter is settled for the Lutherans!)

4. "...*lest Satan tempt you because of your lack of self-control*" (1 Cor. 7:5). Great sex in marriage is spiritual warfare. Spiritual warfare is anything a Christian does in the power of God to stop the devil. Satan sticks his foot out to trip everyone he can. His biggest foot is called lust! He has the power to wind up some cute little "cupie doll" or some "prince charming" to do what a spouse won't do.

The prudish spouse who refuses to enjoy sex or who denies joyful acts of foreplay deeply appreciated by the spouse should seriously reconsider his or her ways. With your spouse and a godly counselor, try to work through your fears or hesitancies. If you are not satisfying your spouse, you could be setting a weaker mate up for an immoral fall. True, no excuse for immorality is acceptable in God's eyes. But fear or Victorian attitudes toward healthy sex with one's husband or wife are dangerous even in a Christian marriage.

Husbands and wives not faithful to receive, believe and do what God says about married sex help themselves or their partners fall over that foot, and great is the fall.

Have you ever heard someone say, "All sins are alike"? Well, God disagrees. He says there is no other sin like sexual immorality. Why? Because it is a sin against the sinner's body.

"Flee [run from] immorality. Every other sin that a man [or woman] commits is outside the body, but the immoral man [or woman] sins against his [or her] own body" (1 Cor. 6:18). In spite of venereal disease, this verse is not just referring to the human body, as other sins affect the human body. Immorality is a sin against the body of Christ, the church. Once sexual immorality is accepted by the leadership of any church, it will almost always spread throughout the church's members until God has to bring severe judgment on that church.

Of course, sexual sin is a sin against the human body: More than twenty-five million Americans now have a venereal disease. Annually doctors report six to twelve million new cases of sexually transmitted diseases (not counting AIDS). The number of AIDS cases continues to grow by the millions worldwide. Many a swinger is abandoning the "swing." The warning alarm is ringing loudly: For a sexually immoral person, no matter what age, hell can begin while you're still alive on this earth.

Husbands or wives who do not understand the natural sex needs of their spouses and who don't work to meet their sexual needs, leave them vulnerable to temptation. The sex drive of either spouse may be greater than the other. She should initiate sex whenever she wants it, and he should initiate sex whenever he wants it. (This principle should stand within a loving framework that allows for the possibility that the timing might not be right. If the timing isn't right, quickly schedule and agree on a time for love.)

Bill Gaultiere had a great suggestion for one wife who said she found initiating the sex act with her husband just "too threatening." Bill suggested that she arrange a signal with her husband. If she took an evening bath she was inviting sex. Today this woman takes a lot more evening baths, and her husband says, "She has the skin I love to touch!"

How Long Can This Go On?

Someone has defined an optimist as an eighty-year-old man who gets married and then moves next door to an elementary school.

According to Genesis 5:32 Noah had regular sex with his wife even when he was five hundred years old. And Sarah had sex with Abraham

220

"in his old age" (Gen. 21:2).

In the New Testament old Zacharias still had sex with Elizabeth long after her time of menopause (see Luke 1).

The single most important factor in maintaining an active sex life for the aging husband is his consistency of active sexual expression. In the largest study yet made among the aged—people over seventy—two out of three women and three out of four men still deeply enjoyed sex. Married couples said they had intercourse at least every eleven days.

It is true people over sixty may slow down in their initial sexual response. An erection that may have taken only seconds in younger years may take five to eight minutes to appear, even with direct stimulation. This doesn't mean a man is becoming impotent or that he's losing his sexual ability. It just means his activity level is slowing down. As one doctor put it, "Just because your legs aren't as strong as they were when you were twenty doesn't mean you give up walking or running."

A woman over sixty may find she doesn't lubricate as quickly. Lubrication is the first visible sign of a wife's physical response, and a woman over sixty may take five minutes to respond that way. She may find it necessary to use a medical lubricating substitute. Just don't quit. (Wives of any age may find such a substitute helpful at times.)

Not every climax will be the best ever. Take real delight in pleasing your spouse anyway—without complaint. Don't ever let the devil lie to you that the thrill is going out of your marriage. If at times you don't succeed with a burst of ecstasy, try, try, again.

Often fears of performance abound. Far too many men have the mistaken fear that their penises are too small. Far too many women have the same misguided fear about their breasts. But studies have shown that the size of one's genitals or breasts makes no difference in the ability to enjoy sex.

Pornography and love never go together. Giving your attention to any form of pornography is both condemned and forbidden by God (see James 1:13-15; Jude 7-8). Pornography is not only destructive to the human mind, it can be very misleading. I'm told that crude novels or films can portray the idea that both the husband and wife must climax together. That's plain silly. In fact, many couples find trying to climax together as difficult as trying to sneeze together—and about as rewarding!

About one in ten men suffer from a chronic case of impotency, unable to have or keep a firm erection. See a well-informed, godly doctor if this is your problem. It is usually something that can be cured with his help. Even the worst cases of impotency can be fully restored to total joy with a penile implant. For information on such an implant write to: American Medical Systems, Consumer Information, Department 670, P.O. Box 9, Minneapolis, MN 55440.

Good Sex

Married sex is not a necessary evil but "the hot fudge sundae of marriage." God says so. As Proverbs 5:18-20 tells husbands,

> Let your fountain be blessed,
> And rejoice in the wife of your youth.
> As a loving hind and graceful doe,
> Let her breasts satisfy you at all times;
> Be exhilarated always with her love.
> For why should you, my son, be exhilarated with an
> adulteress,
> And embrace the bosom of a foreigner?

I've heard prudish people say, "Men today are overly occupied with the female breasts." God doesn't agree with the prudes. He says just the opposite! In fact, if a godly husband and wife will keep turning each other on sexually, neither one is going to want another person's body.

Married sex has always been something to look forward to, according to God's Word. Think of Rachel and Leah, arguing over who would next sleep with their husband, Jacob (see Gen. 30:14-24). Thank God, the New Testament opposes polygamy (see 1 Tim. 3:2, 12; Titus 1:6). Two wives are too much!

If you are married you are meant to be so at ease with your spouse that you can, in total privacy together, talk about any subject at all. If sexual needs still seem too embarrassing to either of you, write letters to each other, always being kind and thoughtful if you discuss anything you're not enjoying about your sexual relationship.

Love may make any spouse concerned for a husband or wife's weight problem—or his or her own. Handle such concern with prayer and tender words. If it's your own weight problem, do what you can to lose or gain weight. If it's your spouse, do what you can to help. But any time you criticize any part of your own or your spouse's body, you cruelly and foolishly drive love away. People who criticize their spouse's weight ought to be far more concerned about the fat between their own ears!

Some wives seem to receive more romantic satisfaction from novels and soap operas than from their husbands. If you are hooked on these empty substitutes for real life:

1. Repent and pray for deliverance from the "lust of the eyes" (1 John 2:15-17). Then refocus on God's Word; leave your problem in the Lord's hands; loosen up; laugh. Laughter is like changing a baby's diaper: It doesn't solve problems permanently, but it makes things more acceptable for a while! Laugh, and your husband laughs with you. Yell at him, and you weep alone.

2. Following the biblical principles in the chapter on communication, look for an appropriate time to share your feelings and needs with your husband. Speak "the truth in love" (Eph. 4:15).

3. Prepare for this conversation with specific prayer. If you have been making marriage anything but godly—spiritually, mentally or physically— "repent and turn to God, performing deeds appropriate to repentance" (Acts 26:20). God created your bodies for each other. Turn to Him in prayer and pray about everything, including your sex life. Pray, "Lord, make me more of a lover to my spouse, and help me find everything You've intended in passion and joy between us. Let my spouse and me be like Adam and Eve before the fall." Come together in Jesus' name.

ADVANCE YOUR SPOUSE'S PULSE; DON'T REPULSE YOUR SPOUSE'S ADVANCES!

Questions for Reflection and Discussion

1. As husband and wife, read the Song of Solomon together out loud. Husband, read Solomon's lines. Wife, read the Shulammite's lines. Read together all other parts. Working alone, write one paragraph giving your view of what God is saying in the Song of Solomon about sex in marriage. Share your paragraphs with each other.

2. The major meaning of the word *authority* in the New Testament is "the delegated right to exercise power." A second meaning of the word underlines the first. This second meaning is "protectorate of." Carefully read 1 Corinthians 7:4 and note that "authority" refers to both husband and wife. What does this mean? Paraphrase 1 Corinthians 7:4 in one paragraph.

3. The Bible gives four—and only four—rules for sex in marriage. We've covered them in this chapter, but let me summarize them: (1) Sex is designed exclusively for a husband and wife, completely alone with each other (see Gen. 2:24-25). (2) Sex must be an act of giving, not an act of forcing (see Phil. 2:3-4). (3) No sexual act should be entered into if it offends either spouse (see Eph. 5:22-25). 4) There must be no pain involved (see Gen. 6:13).

Think about your attitude toward sex when you were first married. What factors shaped that attitude? What is your attitude toward sex now? If it has changed, what has brought about that change? In what way has the Bible given you clear direction about sex in marriage? Considering God's four basic rules for sex in marriage, what changes in attitude or practice do you need to make? Lovingly discuss any such changes with your spouse.

Considering what you've read in this chapter, tenderly, lovingly and honestly discuss with your spouse anything you feel he or she could do— or not do—that would increase the joy of your sex life. Memorize Luke 6:38 and 1 Corinthians 7:2.

4. Discuss with your spouse the difference between romance and sex. How do the seven differences between male and female responses discussed in earlier chapters shed light on any differences in your opinions on this subject? List some of the most romantic things you did when you were courting. If possible, try these activities again. Enjoy the results.

5. What would you say to a married man or woman who told you they were "too old for sex"? List at least four reasons why a married couple is never too old to enjoy sex.

Dear Ray,

I am divorced. I didn't want this divorce, and I hate it. I feel like a failure. I've lost my testimony at church. I have stopped going to the women's meetings because I feel like a leper. Yesterday I phoned my husband and told him about the up-coming CBN Marriage Plus conference. He showed a little bit of interest, not much but some, when I told him Pat Robertson would be there. He still watches him faithfully. That confuses me—that my husband acts like a Christian a lot of the time. It wasn't an affair in our case. He just stopped loving me....

Do you honestly believe there is any hope for our future? I want so badly to have God bring him back to me and cause him to love me again. That's why I want to know what I should be doing until I can get him to that conference of yours. Please tell me how to stop the devil from keeping my husband (ex-husband) away from me.

Needing a Ray of Hope

*"For nothing
is impossible with God."*

Luke 1:37

THIRTEEN

How to Raise Your Marriage From the Dead

**WHEN WE DO WHAT WE CAN,
GOD WILL DO WHAT WE CAN'T!**

He was dead. The newspaper had already carried his obituary, and it was sitting on the bottom of a bird cage. But our Lord Jesus Christ came to the dead man's tomb and said, "Lazarus, come forth" (John 11:43). Lazarus rose from the dead a live man (v. 44). Why? Because a word spoken by our Lord Jesus Christ never returns without accomplishing its purpose (see Matt. 8:8-10; 16; et al.).

What happened in John 11 was impossible. But, as I've been saying all through this book, "With men this is impossible, but with God all things are possible" (Matt. 19:26).

I can join Solomon in saying, "Not one word has failed of all His good promise, which He promised..." (1 Kin. 8:56). You wouldn't have the patience to read an account of all of the miracles I've seen in marriages as I've traveled the world with the Marriage Plus seminars. When couples have acted upon the Word, their homes have not only stood against the storms, but God has done exceeding abundantly above all that those couples could ask or think (see Eph. 3:20).

Some readers might call this book simplistic. But since the Lord has canceled more than twelve hundred divorces during Marriage Plus seminars in the past four years, God's Word speaks for itself.

Do you not know? Have you not heard?
The Everlasting God, the Lord, the Creator of the ends of
  the earth
Does not become weary or tired.
His understanding is inscrutable (Is. 40:28).

Sometimes I'm asked, "What if one person in the marriage really wants the marriage to be beautiful, but the spouse is doing everything to make the marriage miserable. Is there anything God can do?" Well, my darlin' Arlyne can answer that question. I can't believe I'm writing this book on marriage! I can't believe I conduct Marriage Plus seminars! Am I not the guy who wanted to divorce her? Am I not the father whose four-year-old was developing an ulcer because I was fighting with his mother? Am I not the guy who nearly left his wife for an eighteen-year-old? Yep! Arlyne was the *only* one in our marriage who believed God could bring a miracle for us. God did!

It isn't hard for me to believe that Jesus Christ raised Lazarus from the dead—because I see Him raise so many marriages from the dead. Divorced couples, even living in separate states, often come to Marriage Plus seminars. By the end of the seminar they've received over a thousand Scripture verses—and their miracle. As our God has done throughout the ages, "He sent His word and healed them, and delivered them from their destructions" (Ps. 107:20). Their "faith comes from hearing, and hearing by the word of Christ" (Rom. 10:17).

Jeremiah 29:11 in the Living Bible is one of our favorite verses. We believe it's for you: "For I know the plans I have for you, says the Lord. They are plans for good and not for evil, to give you a future and a hope." Lay claim to that promise.

Have you ever asked yourself why Jesus Christ "wept" when He was at the funeral of Lazarus (see John 11:35)? Why would our Lord cry when He knew He was about to raise Lazarus from the dead? There are at least three reasons. First, it was the event that marked the end of Christ's public ministry. He'd be crucified within a month, largely because He dared to perform this miracle. In a real sense He was saying farewell to people He loved. Second, He identifies with our grief whenever we are hurting. Christ never mocks your real pain. Mary, Martha and the other Jews gathered at Lazarus's tomb were weeping. You may be weeping as you

228

read this book. Christ weeps with you. But your whole story isn't over yet. My wife could have closed the book on me too soon and the miracle wouldn't have happened. Third, Jesus wept because of the lack of faith among the people: "But some of them said, 'Could not this man, who opened the eyes of him who was blind, have kept this man also from dying?' " (John 11:37). That mindset grieved our Lord. "And without faith it is impossible to please Him, for he who comes to God must believe that He is, and that He is a rewarder of those who seek Him" (Heb. 11:6).

I don't know how much you want to see your marriage healed. Marriages are not *casually* raised from the dead. A spouse can't sit around and say, "Well, if the Lord wants Ray to remain my husband it will happen in due time." A husband or wife who wants to see his or her marriage healed and blessed has to buckle down and act upon God's Word.

I liked the spunky statement of Nancy Reagan: "A woman is like a tea bag. You never know her strength until you drop her in hot water!" Thank God that when my darlin' Arlyne was in hot water with our marriage she didn't let me drown—or jump out because things got too hot.

Please, if you are already a victim of divorce, don't come under condemnation over what I'm saying. If the things I've said in this book were not part of your understanding, and your spouse (through incest, adultery, drug abuse, alcoholism, violence and so on) made life impossible, you may have done all you knew to do to protect your life or your children. You can only live to the light you've been given. Although I give in-depth teaching on the Bible and divorce in the Singles Plus seminars, this is not a book dealing with that issue.

What More Can I Do?

Someone who has read this whole book may yet be saying, "But, Ray, my marriage is a mess. I can understand a lot of things I've been doing wrong with my tongue, my decisions, my spouse. I see God's Word and recognize His promises are true, but what do I do now?"

First let me give you some great news: "No temptation has overtaken you but such as is common to man; and God is faithful, who will not allow you to be tempted beyond what you are able, but with the temptation will provide the way of escape also, that you may be able to endure it" (1 Cor. 10:13).

The Greek word here translated *temptation* is *peirasmos,* which means "a trial or temptation." In straight terms God promises you He will never allow any trial or temptation to come into your life that you won't be capable of going through. He will always provide a way out for you. That is, He will give you a way to keep you sane and safe so that you can endure the trial.

Never compare yourself with anyone else going through a horrible situation. You are not that person. God makes 1 Corinthians 10:13 an individual promise for every believer. God knows how your mind works. He knows how much you, as an individual, can endure. He won't let your trials go beyond your capabilities. You've got His promise on it.

Watch Out for Self-Pity

If there is one sin you have to fight with all your might, it's self-pity. One wife told me, "With my husband, I thought that if at first I didn't succeed, I should cry, cry, again!" Alcohol won't drown your pain, and drugs won't make your troubles float away. God is the only One who can help you. Obedience to Him is what will give you a great marriage. It may start with everything looking dark, but your deliverance from despair will come as you obey Him (see Jon. 2). Nothing else will.

> Woe to my rebellious children, says the Lord; you ask advice from everyone but me, and decide to do what I don't want you to do. You yoke yourselves with unbelievers, thus piling up your sins. For without consulting me you have gone down to Egypt to find aid and have put your trust in Pharaoh for his protection. But in trusting Pharaoh, you will be disappointed, humiliated and disgraced, for he can't deliver on his promises to save you. For though his power extends to Zoan and Hanes, yet it will all turn out to your shame—he won't help one little bit!...
>
> Yet the Lord still waits for you to come to him, so he can show you his love; he will conquer you to bless you, just as he said. For the Lord is faithful to his promises. Blessed are all those who wait for him to help them (Is. 30:1-5, 18, LB).

Self-pity will stop you from obeying God. That's why our Lord sternly rebuked Peter when he tried to talk Jesus out of going to the cross. In

Matthew 16:23 Jesus turned and said to Peter, "Out of my sight, Satan! You are a stumbling block to me; you do not have in mind the things of God, but the things of men" (NIV). So don't let women's lib or your best friend talk you into feeling sorry for yourself. Ask God for a mature Christian prayer partner (a woman for a woman, a man for a man). His or her purpose isn't to give you pity-parties, but rather godly counsel and needed prayer.

Spend time in your prayer closet—a place where you can be all alone and pray. Cry out to God. Cry! Men, do this too. Let God know, husband or wife, that the emotional pain you are carrying in your marriage is too heavy for you. Give it to God. Stay in prayer for as long as you need. Wait until He lifts the burden. It's time you turned everything over to the Lord.

"I want you to trust me in your times of trouble, so I can rescue you, and you can give me glory" (Ps. 50:15, LB).

Avoid Anxiety Attacks

"Be anxious for nothing, but in everything by prayer and supplication with thanksgiving let your requests be made known to God. And the peace of God, which surpasses all comprehension, shall guard your hearts and your minds in Christ Jesus" (Phil. 4:6-7).

In the seminars I often hear two fears from frustrated wives: "I think I'm going to have a heart attack." Or, "I think I'm going to lose my mind." But God promises to protect your heart and mind if you'll quit your anxious fears and pray about everything. In fact, the Greek word translated *guard* in Philippians 4:7 means that God will "set up sentry duty" over your heart and mind. The Lord is saying, "You don't have to worry that problems will be too big to bear. If anything comes your way that you just can't handle, I will be on guard at the doors of your heart and mind and send the problem away. I won't let it in." Believe God for that.

Note that Philippians 4:6 tells you to pray "with thanksgiving." There are two times to praise the Lord: when you feel like it and when you don't feel like it. Mark 11:24 promises, "Therefore I say to you, all things for which you pray and ask, believe that you have received them, and they shall be granted you." God wants to give you a good marriage, and that's why you can always praise Him in advance.

The word *supplication* in Philippians 4:6 indicates that what you are praying about may take time to accomplish. It's the idea behind Jesus' statement in Luke 18:1b (Amplified), "...they ought always to pray and not turn coward—faint, lose heart and give up."

What you should do until the miracle you are looking for in your marriage really happens is summarized in 1 Peter 5:6-7 (Amplified):

> Therefore humble yourselves (demote, lower yourselves in your own estimation) under the mighty hand of God, that in due time He may exalt you. Casting the whole of your care—all your anxieties, all your worries, all your concerns, once and for all— on Him; for He cares for you affectionately, and cares about you watchfully.

A tearful wife came forward at one of my very first seminars. Tears are a real part of human expression, and she was carrying a tremendous burden. "I've lost my mission field," she said. She explained that she had sung for a well-known singing group. In the height of her career she had met the Lord. Born again, she had begun singing solos in churches. Then (the sobbing began again as she said this), "I got married!"

When the tears began to dry, I asked her, "But why would getting married cause you to lose your mission field?"

She answered, "He doesn't want me to sing in churches anymore. He wants me to stay home and cook his dinner."

I hid a chuckle and explained that most men do think the wife should stay home and cook the meals. "But," I added, "is your husband a Christian?"

"No," she said.

In my spirit I groaned. She had been unequally yoked with an unbeliever, violating 2 Corinthians 6:14, and only the mercy of God could help her now. I told her, "It's not surprising your husband doesn't want you to sing in churches. He doesn't know the Lord, and it makes no sense to him why you'd want to sing for Jesus Christ. The carnal mind doesn't understand spiritual things. You've sinned terribly in knowingly marrying an unsaved man. Now you've got just one way to work things out, and you're going to have to understand this if you're ever really going to be happy again: You haven't lost your mission field. You've just been reassigned. Your husband is now your mission field."

I continued, "I know it may seem strange that God would call you out of a flourishing ministry to minister to just one man. But it happened during the first century. The 'Billy Graham' of Luke's day was named Philip. Luke wrote about him in Acts. Philip preached so well he was turning the whole city of Samaria right side up. But right in the midst of that revival God snatched Philip out of that crowd and stuck him on the backside of a desert where he could minister to one Ethiopian eunuch. Your husband is at least equal to a eunuch!" At that remark she laughed.

She asked, "Do you really believe that what you've taught will get my husband saved?"

I answered, "Obeying God's Word is your only hope."

She went home, acted upon God's Word to the best of her ability, and six months later her husband was saved. They started a ministry together—with him sharing his testimony and her singing in churches.

There is a postscript to this story. This husband was a policeman. Several years ago he was killed in the line of duty. The wife wrote me of her sorrow, also saying, "Think where he'd be now if I had never realized he was my mission field."

Make your husband or wife—whether saved or lost—your mission field. Minister your love. Husband, be the godly head of your home. Wife, "submit to your husband...as to the Lord" (Eph. 5:22). As you do this, your family will *be* Christ's witnesses (see Acts 1:8).

"Don't hide your light! Let it shine for all; let your good deeds glow for all to see, so that they will praise your heavenly Father" (Matt. 5:15-16, LB). People will beat a path to your door trying to find your secret. Then you can share your "secret," as Arlyne and I have shared with you in this book. Tell them Jesus Christ and acting upon the Word of God will give them a *Marriage Plus!*

**GOD WILL NEVER ALLOW ANYTHING TO COME
YOUR WAY THAT YOU AND HE
CAN'T HANDLE TOGETHER!**

Questions for Reflection and Discussion

1. Meditate on and memorize 1 Kings 8:56; Psalm 107:20; Matthew 7:24-25; John 15:7; and Romans 10:17. How does each verse relate to the desires you have for your own marriage? What place does the Bible have in your life?

2. Have you ever felt God was indifferent toward you and your marriage? Have you ever believed He simply couldn't understand your circumstances? Meditate on Isaiah 40:27-29; John 8:31-32; and 1 Corinthians 10:13. Where do thoughts about God's indifference come from? (See John 10:10 and John 8:44.) Finally, meditate on and heed Jeremiah 29:11-13. Memorize these verses.

3. When you are discouraged, meditate on and act on Hebrews 11:1; James 1:2-4; and Philippians 4:6-7.

4. Meditate on and memorize Mark 11:22-26 and 1 Peter 5:6-7. For powerful prayer notice the necessity to forgive and to humble yourself before God. The one who is humble will "in due time" be exalted by God. How important is prayer in your life?

5. Have you ever thought of your spouse and children as your mission field, whether they know the Lord or not? God says they are. Stand on and memorize these verses: 1 Corinthians 7:14; Proverbs 22:6; 1 Peter 3:1-2; and Ephesians 5:25-27. The key to everything shared in this book is Matthew 7:24-27. Will you act upon God's Word?

If the Lord has used this book to bring cancellation to your plans for divorce, please phone or write Arlyne and me and let us know so that we can rejoice with you. Phone Marriage Plus at 818-882-9424, or write us at: Marriage Plus, P.O. Box 4105, Chatsworth, CA 91313.

Notes

Chapter Five

1. Rosenthal, Robert. Harvard University study, written about in *Sensitivity to Non-Verbal Communication* (Baltimore: Johns Hopkins University Press, 1979).
2. Dobson, James. *What Wives Wish Their Husbands Knew About Women* (Wheaton, Ill.: Tyndale House, 1981). Used by permission.

Chapter Six

1. Zinmeister, Karl. "Hard Truths About Day Care," *Reader's Digest.* October 1988, pp. 88-93.
2. Hertz Corporation Headquarters, 225 Brae Boulevard, Parkridge, NJ 07656.
3. Amos, Gary. *Government by the Book* (unpublished manuscript), Regent University, Virginia Beach, Va.

Chapter Seven

1. Brandt, Henry. *Balancing Your Marriage* (Wheaton, Ill.: Scripture Press, 1966), pp. 24-25.

Chapter Eight

1. Barclay, William. *The Letters to the Galatians and Ephesians* (Philadelphia: The Westminster Press, 1976), p. 199.

Chapter Nine

1. Taylor, A. "Why Women Managers Are Bailing Out," *Fortune* Magazine. August 18, 1986, pp. 16-19.
2. Intrater, Keith. *Covenant Relationships* (Shippensburg, Penn.: Destiny Image).

Chapter Ten

1. Barclay, William. *The Letters of James and Peter* (Philadelphia: The Westminster Press, 1976).
2. Barclay, *The Letters of James and Peter*.

Chapter Twelve

1. Domestic Violence Learning Center, Marilyn Post, 2028 Broadway, Quincy, Illinois.
2. Intrater, *Covenant Relationships*.

For full information about live Marriage Plus seminars and Singles Plus seminars or for a full catalog of audio and video tapes of these seminars and other powerful messages by Ray and Arlyne Mossholder, write to:

Marriage Plus
P.O. Box 4105
Chatsworth, California 91313
Phone: 818-882-9424